A CONCISE HISTORY OF THE EUROPEAN UNION

European integration has many origins, although its history goes back less far than is often assumed. This study offers an accessible and engaging overview of the past and present of today's European Union, from the post-war era to the present day. Beginning with the foundational treaties of the 1950s, the book examines how the EU became an increasingly global actor in the course of the 1980s and 1990s. Focusing particularly on recent developments, Kiran Klaus Patel explores how the EU's current role was far from a given and remains fragile. Looking beyond public discourse fixated on crisis, Patel highlights the adaptability and resilience of the EU. Very often it has turned challenges into opportunities and expanded its own role in the process. Still, these developments have left it rather unprepared for the tests it faces in today's world. This book sheds new light on the past in order to understand the present – and possible options for the future. In the process, it challenges the conventional wisdom of Europhiles and Eurosceptics alike.

Kiran Klaus Patel holds the Chair for Modern History at Ludwig Maximilian University of Munich (LMU), where he also serves as the director of Project House Europe, LMU's centre for interdisciplinary research on the history of contemporary Europe. His teaching and research focus on European and US history. Previous publications include *Project Europe: A History* (Cambridge University Press, 2020).

CAMBRIDGE CONCISE HISTORIES

Cambridge Concise Histories offer general introductions to a wide range of subjects. A series of authoritative overviews written by expert authors, these books make the histories of countries, events and topics accessible to both students and general readers.

A full list of titles in the series can be found at:
www.cambridge.org/concisehistories

A CONCISE HISTORY OF THE EUROPEAN UNION

KIRAN KLAUS PATEL
Ludwig Maximilian University of Munich

Translated by
Meredith Dale

CAMBRIDGE
UNIVERSITY PRESS

Shaftesbury Road, Cambridge CB2 8EA, United Kingdom

One Liberty Plaza, 20th Floor, New York, NY 10006, USA

477 Williamstown Road, Port Melbourne, VIC 3207, Australia

314–321, 3rd Floor, Plot 3, Splendor Forum, Jasola District Centre,
New Delhi – 110025, India

Cambridge University Press is part of Cambridge University Press & Assessment, a department of the University of Cambridge.

We share the University's mission to contribute to society through the pursuit of education, learning and research at the highest international levels of excellence.

www.cambridge.org
Information on this title: www.cambridge.org/9781009717151
DOI: 10.1017/9781009717120

Originally published in 2022 by C.H. Beck as *Europäische Integration: Geschichte und Gegenwart*, written in German by Kiran Klaus Patel
(ISBN 978-3-406-78496-5)
© C. H. Beck 2022

This expanded and updated English edition translated by Meredith Dale
© Kiran Klaus Patel 2026

This publication is in copyright. Subject to statutory exception and to the provisions of relevant collective licensing agreements, no reproduction of any part may take place without the written permission of Cambridge University Press & Assessment.

When citing this work, please include a reference to the DOI 10.1017/9781009717120

First published 2026

A catalogue record for this publication is available from the British Library

Library of Congress Cataloging-in-Publication Data
NAMES: Patel, Kiran Klaus author
TITLE: A concise history of the European Union / Kiran Klaus Patel, Ludwig Maximilian University of Munich.
DESCRIPTION: Cambridge, United Kingdom ; New York, NY : Cambridge University Press, 2026. | Series: Cambridge concise histories | Includes bibliographical references and index.
IDENTIFIERS: LCCN 2025044503 (print) | LCCN 2025044504 (ebook) | ISBN 9781009717113 hardback | ISBN 9781009717151 paperback | ISBN 9781009717120 ebook
SUBJECTS: LCSH: European Union – History |
European federation – History | European cooperation – History
CLASSIFICATION: LCC JN30 .P3894 2026 (print) | LCC JN30 (ebook)
LC record available at https://lccn.loc.gov/2025044503
LC ebook record available at https://lccn.loc.gov/2025044504

ISBN 978-1-009-71711-3 Hardback
ISBN 978-1-009-71715-1 Paperback

Cambridge University Press & Assessment has no responsibility for the persistence or accuracy of URLs for external or third-party internet websites referred to in this publication and does not guarantee that any content on such websites is, or will remain, accurate or appropriate.

For EU product safety concerns, contact us at Calle de José Abascal, 56, 1°, 28003 Madrid, Spain, or email eugpsr@cambridge.org.

CONTENTS

List of Figures	*page* vi
List of Maps	viii
List of Boxes	ix
Acknowledgements	x
List of Abbreviations	xiii

	Introduction	1
1	2,500 Years and Five Minutes	8
2	Under the Radar, 1950–1969	24
3	Transformation by Stealth, 1969–1992	57
4	Seeking Freedom, 1992–2009	95
5	Security First: Course Correction, since 2009	140
	Conclusion	182

Chronology	196
Bibliographical Essay	220
Index	243

FIGURES

1.1 T and O world map, eleventh-century book illustration.	page 8
1.2 Nazi propaganda poster from occupied France during the Second World War.	13
2.1 Front page of the French communist daily *L'Humanité* after the French parliament's rejection of the European Defence Community.	26
2.2 The structure of the European Communities in 1958.	33
2.3 National representatives signing the Treaties of Rome in the Palazzo dei Conservatori in Rome, 25 March 1957.	38
2.4 EEC Commission meeting, 1959.	45
3.1 Cartoon 'EEC Summit', Hanns Erich Köhler, 2 December 1969.	59
3.2 Simone Veil (1927–2017), president of the first directly elected European Parliament, at her inaugural speech, 17 July 1979.	65
3.3 and 3.4 The Court of Justice on the Kirchberg plateau in Luxembourg in 1973 and in 2023.	72
3.5 and 3.6 Margaret Thatcher at the Fontainebleau summit in 1984 and supporting the 'Yes' campaign during the 1975 referendum.	75
3.7 Legal acts adopted by the Council and Commission.	82
3.8 The 'temple' of the Maastricht Treaty (1992).	92
4.1 Euro/dollar exchange rate since 1999.	103
4.2 EU trading partners, 2000–2018.	110
4.3 CAP share of EU budget since 1980.	113

4.4	A project supported by the European Regional Development and Cohesion Funds in the Azores.	122
4.5	Polish tourism poster from 2005 playing on the 'Polish plumber' trope: 'I'm staying in Poland. Come to us!'	133
4.6	Differentiated Europe: an incomplete summary (2000).	136
5.1	The heads of the European Council, the European Parliament, and the European Commission – António Costa, David Sassoli, and Ursula von der Leyen – present the Joint Declaration on the Conference on the Future of Europe on 10 March 2021.	143
5.2	Public debt and debt-to-GDP in selected EU states, 2010.	145
5.3	EU27 real GDP, 1996–2024.	147
5.4	Drawing by Lebanese–Swiss cartoonist Patrick Chappatte, published in a Swiss newspaper, 6 March 2020.	158
5.5	Turnout at European Parliament elections since 1979.	166
5.6	Ratio of world goods exports to GDP since the 1970s.	176
5.7	Evolution of the EU budget, 2000–2024.	180
C.1	Ukrainian President Volodymyr Zelenskyy and European Commission President Ursula von der Leyen during a press conference on 4 November 2023.	186

MAPS

I.1 The European Union, including overseas countries and territories, 2025. *page* 3

2.1 EEC, EFTA, and OEEC member states, 1960. 49

BOXES

I.1	Integration	*page* 6
1.1	The German question	16
1.2	Supranational versus intergovernmental	20
2.1	Fathers of a united Europe or loyal patriots?	28
3.1	A flag for the EU	83
4.1	Designing the euro	97
4.2	The failed Constitutional Treaty	125
5.1	European Stability Mechanism	149
5.2	Strategic autonomy	173

ACKNOWLEDGEMENTS

The author of a general work of this kind necessarily owes great debts to many people. In my case, that means first and foremost the students who took my courses on related topics over the past twenty-five years: at Humboldt University in Berlin, at the European University Institute in Florence, at Maastricht University in the Netherlands, and most recently at Ludwig Maximilian University in Munich. I am also grateful to the many colleagues with whom I have collaborated on this topic over the past two and a half decades. Without those projects and the many detailed research publications, I would never have been able to come up with such a concise treatment.

For feedback on this specific book, I would like to thank Victor Jaeschke, Liesbeth Matzer, Berthold Rittberger, and Thomas Süsler-Rohringer. I am also grateful to my (former) student assistants Clara Ebert, Jonathan Holst, and Frieda Ottmann, and especially Lea Lang, for their support. I profited from the chance to present some of the book's arguments at the universities of Aachen, Agder, Bari, Bologna, Brussels, Cambridge, Freiburg, Helsinki, Krakow, Lausanne, Luxembourg, Milan, Magdeburg, Mainz, Padua, Verona, and Vienna, as well as the European University Institute in Florence, Georgetown University, the Hertie School in Berlin, Canada's McGill University, the Federal University of Minas Gerais in Belo Horizonte, Brazil, Peking

Acknowledgements

University, the Scuola Normale Superiore in Pisa, the Sorbonne in Paris, and the History Teachers' Association of Western Australia in Perth. I would like to thank the colleagues and friends who invited me to these places and am grateful for their thoughts and their feedback. Conversations with practitioners, especially during courses I taught at the German Foreign Office with diplomats from various parts of the world, have been particularly helpful.

The book has also profited from several projects I have been involved in. This holds true for the Centre for Advanced Studies in the Humanities and Social Sciences, 'Universalism and Particularism in Contemporary European History', funded by the German Research Foundation, where I would like to thank my two co-directors, Martin Schulze Wessel and Andreas Wirsching. I would also like to extend my thanks to my teams in my ERC advanced grant project InechO on the afterlife of discontinued international organisations (a very useful counterbalance when working on the history of a forum that exists), to Laurent Warlouzet at Sorbonne University, and to the whole team in our project on the history of the EU's environmental policy, as well as to colleagues and fellows at my university's Project House Europe, again especially to Thomas Süsler-Rohringer for all his logistical support.

This English edition builds on an even shorter book in German, published by C. H. Beck in 2022. But it is a great deal more than a mere translation and includes many new parts, especially on the most recent developments, and a bibliography. Meredith Dale, with whom I have worked for fifteen years on a long list of projects, translated this book from German to English. As always, it was a great pleasure to work with him.

At Cambridge University Press, special thanks go to Liz Friend-Smith who believed in this book from the beginning and steered me wonderfully through the publication process. I am grateful to the whole team at Cambridge for its commitment and friendly professionalism, especially to Rosanna Barraclough and Claire Sissen. I would also like to thank Vidhya Ramamourthy, who managed the book's production. Richard Savage did an excellent job as copy-editor, as did Lea Lang collating the index.

ABBREVIATIONS

CAP	Common Agricultural Policy
CFSP	Common Foreign and Security Policy
CSCE	Conference on Security and Cooperation in Europe
DG	Directorate-General
EC	European Community/European Communities
ECA	Economic Cooperation Administration
ECB	European Central Bank
ECSC	European Coal and Steel Community
ECJ	European Court of Justice
EDC	European Defence Community
EEC	European Economic Community
EFTA	European Free Trade Association
EMS	European Monetary System
EP	European Parliament
EPC	European Political Cooperation
EPF	European Peace Facility
ESM	European Stability Mechanism
EU	European Union
FRONTEX	European Border and Coast Guard Agency
G6	Group of Six
GATT	General Agreement on Tariffs and Trade

List of Abbreviations

GDR	German Democratic Republic
MEP	Member of the European Parliament
NATO	North Atlantic Treaty Organization
OEEC	Organisation for European Economic Co-operation
OECD	Organisation for Economic Co-operation and Development
PiS	Prawo i Sprawiedliwość (Law and Justice Party, Poland)
SEA	Single European Act
UNECE	United Nations Economic Commission for Europe
WEU	Western European Union
WTO	World Trade Organization

Introduction

~

This volume sets out to provide a concise and accessible overview of the history of today's European Union. A brief account of such a sprawling topic obviously cannot be comprehensive. Instead, I hope to lay out the broad sweep of developments, without getting bogged down in the details. These days all the EU's significant moves are documented online, including all its treaties, major decisions, national positions, specific policies, and other technicalities. The institutions themselves provide insights into their ongoing work, often also supplying snapshots of historical developments. These come with their own biases. Even more importantly, there are entire libraries of books on specific policies and the roles of institutional actors such as the European Commission, the Parliament, the Council, and the various member states. Amidst such a wealth of information, it is all too easy to get tangled up in the details. In response, this book seeks to provide a coherent survey of the EU's history for the general reader. I would like to reflect briefly on a couple of the central choices that were involved.

The first has to do with chronology and might seem counterintuitive. The closer the book gets to the present, the more detailed the analysis becomes. Today, the European Union influences ordinary people's lives like no other form of international cooperation. Almost half a billion people live in its member states, now extending geographically from Malta in the south to Lapland in the north; from the Atlantic in the west to the Black Sea in the east (Map I.1). The EU also encompasses a scattering of overseas territories, including the exclaves of Ceuta and Melilla in North Africa and the islands of Réunion in the Indian Ocean and Martinique in the Caribbean. The food Europeans – and others – eat, the conditions under which they work and trade, and the laws of their nation states are all strongly shaped by the EU. The EU has great sway beyond its borders, too, especially on economic matters. This international and increasingly global role is a comparably new phenomenon, even if many studies insist on projecting today's eminence back to earlier periods.

Although the institutional history of today's EU now spans more than seventy years, I argue that European integration only really became a force in its own right over the course of the past four decades. My account takes us back to the original treaties of the 1950s – long seen as the key interest for contemporary histories of the organisation – and even further. Still, I argue that the more recent past matters much more and represents the main justification for writing about the subject at all. The immediate past is untrodden ground for historians, who tend to treat ongoing developments as stuff for social scientists. This book seeks to bridge the gap. While paying due attention to the most recent past, I also consider the longer arc. Otherwise, it would be impossible to identify wider trends and important turning points. In that sense, this is a history of the present. It examines a chapter about which most people know very little.

MAP 1.1 The European Union, including overseas countries and territories, 2025. Credit: https://en.wikipedia.org/wiki/Overseas_Countries_and_Territories_Association#/media/File:EU_special_territories_(en).svg.

Secondly, I contend that for a very long time the EU's rise to its present importance was highly improbable – which makes it all the more exciting to uncover the reasons behind that development and to ask how this history will continue. The EU finds itself increasingly under pressure and its future is wide open. In a sense, we are examining history as it is made. The analysis continues to this day. I am acutely aware of the problems involved in contextualising ongoing events, where we lack historical distance. I accept the risk that some parts might quickly appear dated. That is the price of demonstrating the relevance of history in our own times. The gain is historical knowledge in a form relevant to current issues. Looking beyond a public discourse fixated on crisis, I highlight the EU's adaptability and resilience, as well as the new fundamental challenges it faces in our own time. Very often it has been able to turn challenges into opportunities – and to expand its own role in the process. Whether this was always to the benefit of its own citizens (or of those beyond its shores) is another question. Rather than presenting normative judgements, I hope to provide the reader with a firm understanding of this important chapter in Europe's recent history, a basis upon which to make up one's own mind.

Thirdly, the book concentrates on the institutional developments that shaped the European integration process and their effects on wider society, showing how these changed over time. My interest lies less in the motives and ideas of prominent personalities than in the processes that moulded Europe's political landscape and what European integration meant for people within and beyond the member states. Traditionally historians have tended to concentrate on the level of ideas and the nitty-gritty of negotiations. That is undeniably useful, given the complexity of multilateral negotiating processes. This book opts for a different approach, seeking to uncover the larger trends and patterns that have often gone unnoticed. The analysis advances chronologically, while I am acutely aware of the problem of teleology: the tendency to write history backwards, to explain the beginnings in terms of the end. Causalities of that nature are always over-simplistic. While European integration has displayed a considerable path dependency, not least due to its institutions and law, the future was always open. The following chapters therefore pay special attention to turning points, such as the 1970s and the late 2000s, where the trajectory of European integration changed direction. And they take a step back from the powerful narratives that EU institutions have produced about their own past. Rather than a tidy story of progress or decline, I outline the EU's incremental gain in influence – giving due attention to counter-tendencies, inconsistencies, and the universalist and particularist dimensions. Only plural histories can do justice to the complexity of the subject.

Fourthly, a book of this nature is by necessity highly selective and must build heavily on the work of others. Providing a comprehensible and readable account of such a technical topic presents its own set of challenges. Each chapter contains snapshots with more detailed information on a person, a specific moment, or an issue, along with illustrations that offer additional insights and make the reading more lively. While remaining concise, I seek to steer well clear of dry abstraction and unreasonable generalisation. European integration has sparked enormous academic interest, especially among political scientists, legal scholars, and historians. So, the present contribution can draw on a broad range of primary sources and scholarship, with a bibliographical essay surveying the wider scene. The referenced articles and books encompass the multilingual nature of historical research on the EU, reflecting the continent's diverse past and present. Most of all, I hope that this book will serve as a starting point for more detailed exploration of specific issues, and that it will familiarise readers with rival and alternative interpretations. In other words, it should be a starting point for deeper engagement with the history of the European Union.

Hoping that this contribution may also be of use in teaching contexts, I conclude each chapter with a series of questions that might help to start conversations – even if they are by no means exhaustive. While the questions are chapter-specific, it will be helpful to have read the whole book.

A few lines on terminology are warranted. In the context of the process leading up to today's EU, the term 'integration' is not unproblematic. But the same is true of alternatives such as 'cooperation' or 'unification'. I have chosen to use 'integration' to describe the developments at stake – fully aware that the word's history is itself part of the history I describe (Box I.1).

Box I.1 Integration

A word of Latin origin, long marginal in the context of political history. In the early post-war period those pushing for a united Europe based on cooperation among equals often spoke about federalising and unifying the continent, rather than integration. The term first cropped up in debates about the Marshall Plan, the American post-war recovery programme for the western European economies.

It was associated in particular with Paul G. Hoffman, the US Administrator of the Economic Cooperation Administration (ECA), which oversaw the Marshall Plan. In a speech in October 1949, Hoffman pushed the Europeans to liberalise their trade and create a common market. He chose his words carefully: 'integration' was rather vague and avoided the sovereignty-compromising connotations of terms such as unification. In the end the Marshall Plan failed to fulfil the more far-reaching expectations and the term migrated onwards, ultimately finding itself increasingly applied to the European Communities (EC)/EU.

The person who most probably actually coined the term was Miriam Camps, an American economist who was successively involved in several European international organisations. Largely forgotten today, Camps was one of the comparatively few female experts to play a significant role in the EU's male-dominated early years.

The term offers several advantages for scholarship. It is more open than some of the alternatives and devoid of the teleology of contenders such as 'federation'. It is also a reminder of the important role of the United States, especially in the early stages. European 'integration' suggests a non-hierarchical form of cooperation between existing nation states that treat each other (at least formally) as equals.

I

2,500 Years and Five Minutes

~

There are many ways to imagine Europe and the world. Through the Middle Ages the idea of 'Europe' was non-existent for most people. The term only cropped up occasionally in the very small scholarly circles. One important instance was the T and O map illustrated below (Figure 1.1). It was based on the writings of the seventh-century scholar Isidore of Seville (c. 560–636), who described three known continents: Europe, Asia, and Africa. The Mediterranean, the Nile, and the Don form

FIGURE 1.1   T and O world map, eleventh-century book illustration.

the T, separating the three continents from one another, while the O is the encircling ocean. T and O maps were typically displayed 'east up' with Jerusalem at the centre as the navel of the world. Obviously, the cartography was shaped more by religious ideas than literal geography. It is a very long stretch from such notions to the European Union of today – even if they do already contain the idea of Europe as a specific entity. The T and O map reminds us that today's European Union is a very young entity, predicated principally on the history of the twentieth and twenty-first centuries.

1.1 Europe before 'Europe'

European integration is a much more diverse and recent matter than one might think. It was not until the twentieth century that the idea of 'Europe' acquired any meaningful place in ordinary people's lives. This was not a vision that mobilised the masses. That might seem surprising, given that the word itself dates back to antiquity. The Europa of Greek mythology was the Phoenician princess whom Zeus, disguised as a bull, abducted and took to Crete. The word's geographical sense is equally ancient. For example, when the Greek historian Herodotus wrote about Europe in the fifth-century BCE, he was referring to the region in which he himself lived, distinguishing the civilised Greeks from their allegedly barbarian adversaries, the Persians. While Herodotus asserted that Europe was larger than the other two known continents, Asia and Africa, his real geographical knowledge was restricted to Greece and what is now southern Italy. From Roman times through most of the Middle Ages the term largely disappeared. All in all, Europe remained a vague and marginal concept.

It was in the twelfth and thirteenth centuries that the word 'Europe' began reappearing in various European languages, frequently in connection with conflicts and crises such as the Crusades and the Ottoman expansion. European peace projects have cropped up sporadically ever since. The birth of the idea of European integration is often traced to the late Middle Ages, citing a venerable lineage including Dante Alighieri as well as early modern writers such as the Duke of Sully and Immanuel Kant. However, ideas such as these remained highly marginal and were discussed only in select elite circles. In fact, some of the crucial texts were completely forgotten for long periods. William Penn's *Towards the Present and Future Peace of Europe* of 1693, for example, was originally published in very small numbers, and the few surviving copies gathered dust in libraries for almost two hundred years. The text was rediscovered in the nineteenth century, as intellectuals began to explore how the states of Europe could coexist in peace – and might even eventually unite as equals – in response to the emergence of nation states and the wars associated with that process. Thinkers like Victor Hugo and revolutionaries like the Italian Giuseppe Mazzini and his Hungarian friend Lajos Kossuth exalted the idea of Europe. But even in the nineteenth century such debates were of little relevance to most people.

On the other hand, the continent had always been a place of cross-border exchange of ideas, goods, and people. By the Middle Ages the region we now call Europe was united by cooperation and competition, by strivings for independence and attempts to unify it peacefully or by force. But

1.1 Europe before 'Europe'

there were also strong connections to other parts of the world, such as Africa and Asia. Commerce and ideas – as well as violent conquest and domination – formed connections far beyond Europe's shores, as more recent scholarship has underlined. 'Europe' was not as clearly defined as it is today. The idea that the Urals form a geographical boundary, for example, dates from the eighteenth century, when Russia was asserting its identity as a major European power. Europe's margins were fuzzy and, equally importantly, integration initiatives never encompassed the entire continent. Conversely, through colonialism and imperialism, parts of Europe had closer ties to overseas territories than within their own continent. In other words, Europe was constructed, and for most of history 'Europeans' never gave a thought to 'Europe'.

Only after the devastation of the First World War did the concept of Europe and European integration gradually become relevant to broader sections of the population, with the emergence of ideas about political and economic cooperation. The advocates of non-hegemonic forms of European cooperation now connected across borders more than ever before. But there were still narrow limits to mobilisation and participation: Europe remained a project of the elites. Take Count Richard Coudenhove-Kalergi's Paneuropa Union of the 1920s, which employed modern methods of mass communication and claimed to be seeking broad mobilisation. In reality the Austrian count was primarily interested in prominent aristocrats, politicians, and business leaders, and the organisation's international membership never exceeded a few thousand.

The interwar efforts of political leaders fared little better. On 5 September 1929 French Foreign Minister Aristide

Briand proposed 'some kind of federal link' for Europe constructed around Franco-German reconciliation.[1] Berlin was not interested. German Foreign Minister Julius Curtius said Briand's proposal would be given 'a first-class burial'.[2] And he was nowhere near Germany's most fervent nationalist at the time. Fundamentally doomed in the poisoned political climate of the late 1920s, the French initiative was eclipsed within weeks by the Wall Street Crash. Relations within Europe were soon to be determined by economic autarchy and violent nationalism.

Nascent engagement for European peace and reconciliation was crushed by reaction and fascism. Still, the debate about Europe continued. In some cases, even the extreme right instrumentalised the concept of Europe – generally to elevate their particular nation over all others. In Germany, the Nazis exploited this trope, for example when Reich Foreign Minister Joachim von Ribbentrop spoke in November 1941 of the 'solidarity of our destiny'. The Axis fighting the Soviet Union was, he said, a 'shining example of the already existing and constantly growing moral unity of Europe'.[3] Of course this was but

---

[1] The text of Briand's proposal is available online at https://sgae.gouv.fr/files/live/sites/SGAE/files/Contributed/SGAE/02_Tout-Savoir_UE/documents/Discours%20d%27Aristide%20Briand%20le%205%20septembre%201929.pdf; for his more detailed ideas from 1930, see: www.europarl.europa.eu/100books/file/EN-N-B-0014-Memorandum.pdf (both accessed 1 May 2025).

[2] Karl Dietrich Erdmann, ed., *Akten der Reichskanzlei, Kabinette Brüning I/II*, vol. 1 (Boppard am Rhein: Harald Boldt Verlag, 1982), Doc. 68, Meeting of Ministers, 8 July 1930, p. 283.

[3] Joachim von Ribbentrop, Speech, 26 November 1941, in Walter Lipgens, ed., *Documents on the History of European Integration*, vol. 1 (Berlin: Walter de Gruyter, 1985), doc 16, quote p. 91 (English), German original on a microfiche that is part of Lipgens's publication.

1.1 Europe before 'Europe'

FIGURE 1.2 Nazi propaganda poster from occupied France during the Second World War. It encourages Frenchmen to join the Waffen SS.

a transparent ruse to mobilise support during a period when the fate of the war was turning against Nazism, and Ribbentrop's ideas had nothing to do with cooperation between equals. Hitler disapproved anyway, and his regime never flinched from its course of anti-Semitism, racial superiority, and militarism. Although pan-European propaganda from the far right remained a marginal phenomenon, it does explain why post-1945 pro-European sloganeering sometimes touched a raw nerve, especially when it came from Germany (Figure 1.2).

All kinds of ideas emerged during and in response to the Second World War. The exiled German author Stefan Zweig mourned in 1942: 'Europe, the homeland of my heart's choice, is lost to me',[4] destroyed by the two world

---

[4] Stefan Zweig, *The World of Yesterday: An Autobiography* (German original: 1941) (Lincoln: University of Nebraska Press, 1964), p. xviii.

13

wars. And discussions about a European future emerged within the resistance, currents proposing Europe as the answer to the crises that had delegitimised the pre-war political models. Activists like the Italian Communist Altiero Spinelli saw the *tabula rasa* left by the war as a chance to create a federal Europe without nation states. Such voices were rather marginal at the time, and most people were simply busy surviving the war. Until 1945 Europe therefore remained one *possible* future – but an extremely unlikely one.

1.2 Trial and Error

In the beginning was the war. Without the Second World War – without the destruction, the discrediting of extreme nationalism, the dismantling of Europe's global dominance, and the fear of further German aggression – European integration would never have segued from the sphere of the thinkable to the realm of the politically doable.

All the same, the road ahead remained rocky. The hopes of federalists like Spinelli – that a united federal Europe could be achieved immediately – came to nought. Instead, the political agenda was dominated by reconstruction of the nation states, which most Europeans now valued even more highly after the experience of fascism, war, and Soviet expansion. But this was not simply a resurrection of the pre-war form of statehood. The new polities were to be embedded more deeply in international structures. Alongside new ideas about global collaboration and emerging superpower blocs, various European regional models proposed closer cooperation in the North Atlantic space, among the Benelux states or in the

Nordic context. In south-eastern Europe the Yugoslav leader Josip Broz Tito launched a short-lived initiative for a socialist Balkan federation. Across the board Europe was gaining momentum, even if it was not yet clear where it was heading.

This specific context, in which neither nation states nor empires seemed to serve Europe's international governance needs, made the idea of some kind of European union a plausible political option. To the Western powers in an increasingly divided Europe, four motives were central. Firstly, peace had to be secured after two devastating world wars. Secondly, the German question (Box 1.1) had to be solved: that meant finding a viable arrangement for a defeated, occupied, and divided country (or at least its western sectors). Thirdly, economic recovery was needed to boost prosperity. And fourthly, Europe had to find its place in a world increasingly divided between two emerging superpowers, the United States and the Soviet Union. None of these motives were new, least of all the desire for peace and the wish to project power. 'Never again!' should extreme nationalism and isolationism be permitted to drag the continent – and the world – into the abyss. Cooperation and integration were regarded as the best medicine. Proposals like those of Coudenhove-Kalergi and Briand appear prescient in retrospect, their concrete approaches visionary: Franco-German reconciliation, strict anti-communism, and the idea of harnessing capitalist economic systems for political ends. A marginal dimension from the past now offered blueprints for the future.

But this was not yet the starting shot for the EU. Instead, the first five post-war years saw the emergence of a veritable labyrinth of international organisations

Box 1.1 The German question

The German question originated in the nineteenth century, during the period when Europe's modern nation states emerged. Essentially it was about the borders and political organisation of Germany, which was becoming Europe's major land power. At the beginning of the nineteenth-century Germany was composed of a multitude of states and statelets. Many Germans lived outside their borders, many non-Germans within them. Not until 1871 were they united to form a cohesive political entity encompassing most of the historically German lands with Prussia at the helm. Germany rapidly became a powerful empire with colonies in various parts of the world. The two world wars led to substantial territorial losses in the first half of the twentieth century. Politically, the country underwent fundamental changes: from monarchy to democracy in 1918–1919 and then the Nazi dictatorship (1933–1945). After military defeat in 1945 Germany was divided into four zones of occupation, one for each of the four victorious Allied powers. In 1949 the former British, French, and American zones formed the Federal Republic of Germany with Bonn as its capital, while the Soviet zone in the east became the German Democratic Republic. The issue now – the 'German question' of the post-war era – was how to ensure that Germany (or at least its western half) could recover economically without posing a threat to its neighbours. And as the Cold War confrontation heated up, West Germany's industrial output and military support were in demand. In the end, all these factors drew West Germany into the Western institutional frameworks.

seeking to foster European cooperation, sometimes overlapping, sometimes competing. The first of these, the United Nations Economic Commission for Europe (UNECE, founded in 1947), was pan-European and even included both superpowers. The Cold War confrontation soon shunted it to the sidelines. Then there were organisations founded to banish the ghosts of the past and guarantee security in a dangerous world. One such, directed principally against Germany and the Soviet Union, was the Western Union founded by Belgium, France, Luxembourg, the Netherlands, and the United Kingdom in 1948, which became the Western European Union (WEU) in 1954. The year 1948 was also when the Organisation for European Economic Co-operation (OEEC, later, from 1961, the Organisation for Economic Co-operation and Development, OECD) emerged from the US-led Marshall Plan. The Council of Europe, focusing more on human rights, followed in 1949.

There were dozens more, often concerned with specifically economic or rather technical problems such as infrastructure. Since the nineteenth-century Europe had accumulated a wealth of experience in international cooperation, regulating matters like navigation on the Rhine and the Danube, postal cooperation, or the establishment of international rail and telegraph networks. Some of those involved, like French economist Michel Chevalier, argued that transnational infrastructure projects could help build peace in Europe. These discussions gained further momentum during the interwar years, with engineers like Hugo Junkers, Piero Puricelli, and Georges Valensi proposing European unity built on airline networks, motorways, and telecommunications. All in all, these tended to be 'concealed' forms of integration driven by experts. As broader sections of the political elites turned their attention to Europe after 1945, they were able to build on these foundations. That kind of experience with cross-border infrastructure projects and economic cooperation was at least as formative for the trajectory of European post-war integration as thinkers like the Duke of Sully, William Penn, and Immanuel Kant. Europe was not just one big idea, but a confluence of very many very different projects.

By the 1950s internationalisation and globalisation had progressed to a point where the states of Europe no longer represented self-contained units (if they ever had been). The question was only which of the many available European and international governance models they would choose, in a situation where the UNECE, the Council of Europe, and the OECD all claimed to have *the* solution for the continent's problems. So, the international arena was anything but empty when the foundations were laid for what is now the EU. Instead of one Europe, there were already many.

So why create yet another? And what made it special? The earliest direct precursor of today's European Union represented the outcome of the intensive search for a European solution during the first five post-war years. Several aspects had become apparent. Firstly, the brutal reality of the Cold War meant that no pan-European initiative, such as the UNECE, stood the slightest chance. The East–West tensions were increasingly unbridgeable and Europe was not a significant point of reference in the emerging Eastern Bloc's system of Soviet-led internationalism. Countries like Czechoslovakia, hitherto closely connected to western Europe, now found themselves suddenly on the other side of the Iron Curtain; here the Cold War tore apart deeply rooted ties. That is why, politically, 'Europe' meant western Europe for so long. Alongside the Second World War, the Cold War was the defining context for early European integration. Apart from anything, Europe was too weak to operate independently of the two superpowers. Many in post-war Europe would have preferred such a neutral position. But as the East–West conflict deepened, European integration became ever more closely tied to transatlantic cooperation. Washington's security guarantee made it the hegemonic power in western Europe and became one of the determining factors in the European debate from the late 1940s.

Secondly, the Cold War had created another fact on the ground: Germany was divided. 'Europe' had to deal with the western part of the country, which became the Federal Republic of Germany in 1949. Whereas earlier European integration efforts had tended to be adversarial or simply omitted Germany on account of its division and occupation, the question now was West Germany's role in the emerging Western Bloc – especially after it came out of the war less economically weakened than many had expected. Now the European project had to relate to West Germany's growing economic power in the continent's fragile, fragmented heartland.

Thirdly, the discussions up to this point, especially in the Council of Europe framework, had revealed widely diverging ideas about what Europe should look like. Only a handful of countries were able to build on substantial popular support for ceding sovereignty to a new supranational organisation (Box 1.2). Elsewhere, for example in the United Kingdom and the Scandinavian countries, that was out of the question. After all, the United Kingdom had just defeated Nazi Germany.

> **Box 1.2** Supranational versus intergovernmental
>
> European integration has always been based on multiple modes of cooperation. For present purposes the two most important are 'supranational' and 'intergovernmental'. In supranational cooperation, participating states cede certain aspects of their sovereignty to a shared institution with its own powers. Supranational bodies can set their own agenda; their jurisdiction and other decisions are binding on member states. In intergovernmental cooperation, each participating state has a veto and thus retains full sovereignty. The two principles create different constellations of power and imply different forms of decision making. The European Union has always operated on both principles, with the balance between them shifting repeatedly over time.
>
> It is the supranational dimension that makes the EU special. All the other major international organisations are strictly intergovernmental; nowhere else have sovereign nation states ceded so much power to a shared political framework. For this reason, today's EU is a unique experiment in governing a major world region.

Instead, the latter group pursued more intergovernmental forms of cooperation that interfered less with sovereignty and granted every member state a veto. So, where states came together to discuss core aspects of sovereignty it was increasingly clear that the most that could be expected was intergovernmental collaboration, as in the Council of Europe. Anyone seeking closer forms of cooperation therefore needed to make a fresh start, and it was obvious that that would involve fewer states than the UNECE with its eighteen founding members, the OEEC (sixteen), or the Council of Europe (ten).

1.2 Trial and Error

The Schuman Declaration of 9 May 1950 – as the point of origin of today's EU – stood at the end of this learning curve. It was, nevertheless, as French Foreign Minister Robert Schuman himself admitted, 'a leap into the unknown'. Concretely he argued for a European authority to pool coal and steel production: his proposal 'that Franco-German production of coal and steel as a whole be placed under a common High Authority' would 'make it plain that any war between France and Germany becomes not merely unthinkable, but materially impossible'. For Schuman, cooperation in these militarily crucial sectors was inseparably bound up with the question of peace. He also tied reconciliation with the young West Germany to an invitation to other western European states to join the project of 'de facto solidarity'.[5] All this built on interwar discussions: the bond of anti-communism, the idea of harnessing the economy to political ends, and the Franco-German core all predated the Second World War. Yet Schuman's plan was also genuinely visionary. For the first time France was extending its hand to the young Federal Republic (West Germany), offering a partnership of equals just five years after the end of the war. Konrad Adenauer, West Germany's towering chancellor, immediately recognised the far-reaching implications of Schuman's speech. Defending the plan in the Bundestag, he stressed the 'political significance of the proposal' and its potential 'to eliminate differences between our two nations that

---

[5] Brent F. Nelsen and Alexander Stubb (eds.), *The European Union: Readings on the Theory and Practice of European Integration*, 3rd edition (Houndmills: Palgrave Macmillan, 2003), all quotes p. 14.

have persisted for centuries'.[6] Tactically it was astute to target two key industrial sectors while steering clear of the most sensitive spheres of state power such as foreign policy and security. That certainly helped to blunt national objections to European solutions.

At the same time the idealism of the proposal should not be overstated. The French government only arrived at this position after all other attempts to contain Germany politically had failed. Economic interests mingled into the geostrategic motives. Efforts to modernise French industry had faltered and the coal and steel sectors suffered wider structural problems. The idea was that integration would constrain the considerably stronger West German economy in these two key sectors before it could unfold its full potential.

The trigger for Schuman's speech was a move by France's wartime allies. The United Kingdom and the United States wanted to lift the restrictions that capped West Germany's annual steel production at 11.1 million tonnes. That decision was due for 10 May 1950, the day after Schuman's speech. In a situation of escalating East–West tensions – just weeks before the outbreak of the Korean War – London and Washington were pressing for rearmament, even if that meant strengthening West Germany. That was not in France's interest. It was in this problematic context that Schuman made his move. The originator of the plan was in fact Jean Monnet, soon to become the *éminence grise* of the European integration process. Of course, Schuman and Monnet really did want

---

[6] Deutscher Bundestag, *Stenographische Berichte der Verhandlungen des Deutschen Bundestags*, 68th session, 13 June 1950, p. 2460.

to avoid another war in Europe, above all another war with Germany. But integration also offered an innovative and attractive instrument for securing French predominance in western Europe's emerging post-war order. The most visionary thing about the Schuman plan was its focus on the feasible, while linking national interests to European objectives was a stroke of genius. Schuman's speech lasted about five minutes. In 1950 no one could have guessed how those five minutes were to change the continent's history.

Questions

1. How important were medieval and early modern ideas about European peace for post-1945 European integration initiatives?
2. Discuss how the Nazis and other fascists employed the concept of Europe during the 1930s and 1940s.
3. What distinguished the initial processes that led to today's European Union from other post-1945 attempts to foster cooperation across the continent?

2

Under the Radar, 1950–1969

2.1 A New Start

The governments of France, West Germany, Italy, and the three Benelux states signed the treaty establishing the European Coal and Steel Community (ECSC) in Paris in April 1951, just eleven months after Schuman's declaration. Labelling this grouplet 'European' suggests no lack of confidence. No existing organisation was dissolved; instead, the UNECE, OEEC, Council of Europe, WEU, and ECSC were rather like a set of Russian matryoshka dolls, with the ECSC – as the predecessor of today's EU – the smallest and newest. At the time there was no telling what it would grow into.

The ECSC of 1951 set out with great expectations. But its remit was too limited to actually play any meaningful role in higher spheres like peace and prosperity. Even more crucially, its core mission – to dismantle trade barriers and create a common market and common policies for coal and steel – was very quickly thrown off course. A slump in demand for coal in the period 1957–59 threw a spanner in the works as its member states prioritised their national interests. West Germany imposed a moratorium on coal imports, certainly violating the spirit if not the letter of the ECSC's treaty. The Netherlands and Italy openly flouted the community preference rules and purchased cheap American coal. So much for the 'de facto solidarity' invoked by Schuman in 1950.[1] Global markets and international politics trumped the ECSC rulebook. As we shall see, that dynamic was to recur many, many times in the course of the integration process.

That is not to say that the ECSC was passive. The coal crisis saw a lot of talk – but little action. As so frequently in the integration process, the ECSC diverted its attention to other areas such as social housing and research, with notable medium-term outcomes. Nevertheless, the limits of this structure were clear: this new Europe fell well short of expectations.

But that is only half the story. Even before the ECSC was up and running its member states were thinking about the next steps. In the very week the official negotiations for the ECSC began, North Korean forces crossed the border into South Korea on 25 June 1950. The Korean War, as one of the major armed conflicts of the Cold War, catapulted the question of German rearmament to the top of the political agenda. Paris, which had blocked the idea not least for historical reasons, now bent to US pressure – but proposed a path that appeared politically less unpalatable than creating a West German army under Bonn's command. In October 1950, French Prime Minister René Pleven proposed the creation of a European army, drawing on ideas put forward by Jean Monnet and repurposing the organisational model of the ECSC. Bonn, Rome, and the Benelux states all signed up to the European Defence Community (EDC), and the six

---

[1] Brent F. Nelsen and Alexander Stubb, *The European Union* (London: Macmillan, 1994), p. 14.

of the ECSC appeared to be hurtling towards far-reaching integration in a central area of state sovereignty.

In the end it was Paris that hit the brakes. In August 1954, after the complex negotiations had finally been completed, the French National Assembly rejected ratification (Figure 2.1). As well as purely domestic doubts and difficulties, recent history weighed heavily. For a majority of French deputies this was a step too far so soon after the end of the war. Accepting West Germany as an equal partner in the ECSC was one thing; agreeing to West German rearmament, even in a European context, quite another. In hindsight those fears might appear

FIGURE 2.1 Front page of the French communist daily *L'Humanité* after the French parliament's rejection of the European Defence Community. The sub-head notes that the deputies celebrated the outcome by singing the French national anthem, 'La Marseillaise'.

exaggerated. At the time, with the wounds so fresh, they certainly made sense.

The collapse of the military project also dragged another initiative down with it. Under Article 38 of the draft treaty for the EDC the six parties also planned to establish a European political community, as an attempt to create a kind of shared constitution for the six member states. This new project, driven especially by the Italian government of Alcide De Gasperi, was to encompass foreign policy powers as well as coal, steel, and defence. The demise of the EDC automatically took this initiative down with it. De Gasperi, who was elected president of the ECSC's Common Assembly in May 1954, died unexpectedly on 19 August, just eleven days before his proposal was shot down. He would certainly have agreed with his successor, the Belgian Paul-Henri Spaak, who called the French vote a 'very heavy blow for the supporters of a united Europe' (Box 2.1).[2]

Any gaps created by the demise of the defence community were plugged without delay, and it was quickly agreed to rearm West Germany within the North Atlantic Treaty Organization (NATO) framework. The chosen vehicle, the Western European Union, had been created in the immediate aftermath of the war as a bulwark against German (as well as Soviet) aggression. It now became the conduit for the country's Western integration. This was actually politically advantageous for West Germany, which was able to acquire a more accepted and influential position in NATO than it would have had in a

---

[2] Paul-Henri Spaak, *Combats inachevés*, vol. 2 (Paris: Fayard, 1969), p. 60 (this section was not included in the book's English version).

Box 2.1 Fathers of a united Europe or loyal patriots?

Leading politicians from the six ECSC member states are often held up as the founding fathers of a unified Europe: Konrad Adenauer, Joseph Bech, Johan Willem Beyen, Alcide De Gasperi, Jean Monnet, and Paul-Henri Spaak, to name but a few. In this reading, they all shared a vision of Europe overcoming past conflicts and pressed for a form of European unity that transcended the nation state. The view that their idealism paved the way for Europe to make a fresh start in the 1950s was enshrined in their own speeches and memoirs and is perpetuated by EU institutions to this day – although the EU has recently attempted to make the list more diverse by including women and figures from states that only joined later.

Research since the 1980s has challenged that idealistic interpretation. Since the relevant archives released the materials relating to the early phase, scholars have identified national interests as the key factor promoting and limiting European integration. According to the historian Alan S. Milward and others, joint decisions only emerged if they served the member states themselves. European policies were thus the outcome of shared or complementary national interests and member states remained in control of the process.

There are good arguments for both these perspectives, and it was often a combination of both that drove European integration. The hope for a more united European future and an alternative to the conflicts of the past did drive political negotiations and helped to legitimise them. At the same time, most of the politicians in charge of the process opposed a complete surrender of national sovereignty. Member states strove to profit from joint initiatives, be it economically or politically, and this explains the many rounds of hard-nosed negotiations and often ambivalent outcomes. And a third dimension must be considered too. It would be wrong to overemphasise the importance of the highest political representatives from the member states. Other players influenced the process too, including powerful economic lobbies and increasingly also the new European institutions themselves. Finally, there were institutional alternatives at the European level, such as the Council of Europe and the OEEC. During the first decades after the Second World War decision makers navigated between these different options and sometimes preferred one of the alternatives. Trial and error emerges as an important factor alongside interests and values.

solely European arrangement. Paradoxically the emphatic French 'Non!' opened up a path for West Germany to create its own armed forces. The idea of securing peace through security thus remained for many decades largely outside the remit of the predecessors of today's EU. At the international level this was NATO's unchallenged role and responsibility. Moreover, the failure of this attempt to expand supranationality in the institutional framework served as a cautionary tale discouraging further such plans.

For France, the bitter pill of West Germany joining NATO was sweetened by the Franco-German counterweight created by the ECSC. The various international organisations functioned like communicating vessels. While NATO took care of security for the Europe of six, the latter provided the alliance with stability and support.

All these talks and transformations went largely over the heads – or explicitly against the wishes – of the public at large. In West Germany in the first half of the 1950s the Social Democratic Party and the trade unions mobilised energetically against rearmament, along with the Protestant Church and prominent intellectuals. But Konrad Adenauer's government paid little heed. Joining the EDC and NATO was controversial, but security considerations came first. Even at this stage, European integration was often unpopular once it became serious and concrete. Some also objected on principle. The French and Italian communists – who at that time held between a quarter and a third of the popular vote – rejected these military plans and condemned them as a US-led capitalist conspiracy against the European working class that deepened the Cold War divide. But even the staunchest supporters of European integration were highly critical: the institutional nitty-gritty frustrated federalists who hoped that a United States of Europe was just around the corner. Politicians such as De Gasperi, Schuman, and Spaak trod a fine line between 'too much' and 'too little' integration.

Despite lukewarm popular support, the proponents of a united Europe quickly found an alternative security arrangement after the EDC debacle. They also began looking more widely for new European opportunities. In the brief period between December 1954 and April 1955 they produced more than fifty ideas for European initiatives, with the High Authority of the ECSC under Jean Monnet particularly prominent as a source of institutional proposals.

Just as the ECSC represented the sum of the lessons of the first five post-war years, the next step drew together and built on the experience the participating governments had accumulated in the ECSC's first half a decade. The ignominious collapse of the defence project revealed the strength of political forces in various member states that baulked at relinquishing core state sovereignty. Others argued that the ECSC could not supply a viable basis for political and economic cooperation in western Europe, so they had to forge ahead. The Benelux states in particular produced a multitude of initiatives, culminating in a conference of the ECSC foreign ministers in early June 1955 in Messina, Italy. Here the six ministers agreed on a rather dry and dull programme of work. They established an intergovernmental committee to examine and develop a series of integration projects in politically less sensitive policy areas, without committing to a supranational approach. The final resolution included several references to the member states' determination to 'go a step further towards the construction of Europe'.[3] While the concrete substance remained deliberately vague, it was clear that they wanted to move forwards together.

Intensive talks over the subsequent twenty-one months also confirmed two priors. First, it had become clear that the United Kingdom – which had been invited to Messina – would not be on board any supranational initiative, and certainly not one that clashed with its global empire. Second, the six had now returned to the path of concentrating on politically less sensitive matters. They agreed to foreground two core issues from the Messina meeting – a common market and the peaceful use of nuclear power – and to prepare a treaty for each. Other policy areas featured within the context of the common

---

[3] Resolution adopted by the Foreign Ministers of the ECSC Member States (Messina, 1 to 3 June 1955), English translation from CVCE, University of Luxembourg, www.cvce.eu/obj/resolution_adopted_by_ the_foreign_ministers_of_the_ecsc_member_states_messina_1_to_3_ june_1955-en-d1086bae-0c13-4a00-8608-73c75ce54fad.html (accessed 1 May 2025).

market programme. Many questions remained highly controversial and were frequently papered over by ambiguity. All in all, the approach was a veritable melange of visionary thinking and pragmatic consensus-seeking. Wherever possible the texts were legally watertight, but where differences could not be bridged the formulations were left deliberately vague. The process was turbulent and often appeared to be on the brink of failure. There was no master plan guiding the new projects; instead, their character reflected the aggregate of the provisional compromises made by the participants.

The outcome of this long and winding process was the Treaties of Rome of 25 March 1957, which created two new Communities: the European Economic Community (EEC) and Euratom. This represented a decisive breakthrough for the ECSC format, even if the two new organisations emerged from the ruins of much grander plans. In organisational terms, they were neither part of the ECSC nor completely separate. Instead, the process created a rather opaque hybrid arrangement. Each of the three had its own commission with executive powers, at least opening a door for supranationality. But the ECSC also featured an intergovernmental Council of Ministers, added during the 1951 treaty negotiations at Belgian and Dutch behest to oversee the executive organ and guard the interests of the member states. The same arrangement was now applied to the EEC and Euratom. In fact, the two new Communities were less supranational than the ECSC and much less than the EDC would have been. But the ECSC, Euratom, and the EEC also shared certain institutions, first and foremost the Court of Justice and the Parliamentary Assembly (which later morphed into the

European Parliament). Both were originally established as part of the ECSC and both would play a vital role in shaping the EEC from the 1960s – although that was certainly not foreseeable in 1957. The Parliamentary Assembly was not a parliament in the sense of a representative body with legislative powers. Its remit was extremely limited. And equally importantly, parliamentary representation was also part of the institutional arrangement of the Council of Europe, the WEU, NATO, and other organisations. So, the European Communities' parliamentary organ was nothing out of the ordinary. Especially in the formative phase the situation of three parallel communities alongside a string of other European organisations led to rivalry and friction. As a result, the process did not *look* like a giant leap towards a united Europe (Figure 2.2).

In terms of policy coverage too, the three European Communities were quite a patchwork. The ECSC was a sectoral intervention permitting its six member states to collectively regulate the coal and steel sectors. Euratom

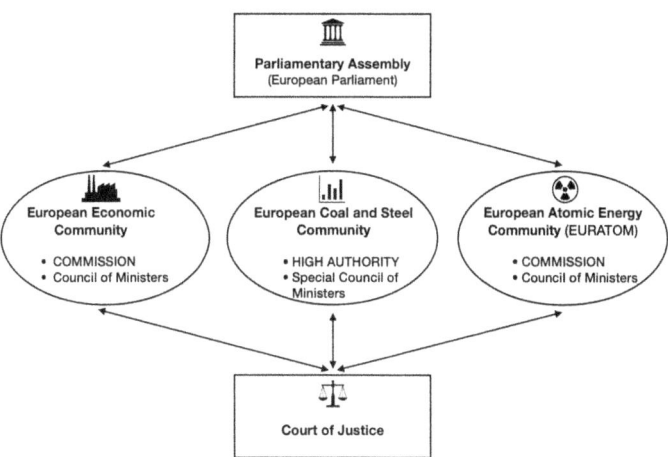

FIGURE 2.2 The structure of the European Communities in 1958.

adopted a similarly sectoral approach in the sphere of nuclear power. But the EEC enjoyed a broader mandate designed to create a common market without internal tariffs, with free movement of goods, persons, services, and capital, and common external trade rules. The EEC treaty also contained vague allusions to other common policies, such as a common agricultural policy and a common transport policy, as well as supporting social policy measures. No one imagined that these three treaties would define the institutional, legal, and administrative parameters of the next four decades of European integration.

Nor was it clear which of the three new treaties was more significant. The senior leaders at the ECSC originally expected to lead the process but were quickly disappointed. Monnet and the French government initially found Euratom more promising than the EEC, especially in light of France's lead in both civil and military nuclear technology. At that time many experts and intellectuals had utopian hopes for atomic energy. Some, like the philosopher Ernst Bloch, saw it as the miracle cure for all future energy needs and social problems. The common market had first been officially proposed by Dutch Foreign Minister Johan Willem Beyen, not least with an eye to securing export markets for his country's own highly competitive export sectors. One of the main issues in the talks was how protectionist or liberal this common market should be. On the basis of general trade patterns and their own weak industrial competitiveness, the French and Italian governments argued for the former; Bonn and The Hague insisted on the latter. Belgium and France wanted the initiative to integrate their colonial empires, while the others showed little interest in shouldering a share of those costs. More broadly though, late colonialism did play an important role in the early phases of European integration. The Netherlands also still had colonies at the time, and even Italy was involved in Somaliland. In the late 1950s few western Europeans yet believed that the colonial era was over.

The EEC is frequently portrayed as a trade-off between Paris and Bonn: France sought agricultural integration; the Federal Republic (West Germany) wanted the Common Market; each accepted the other's demand in order to further their own. That is an oversimplification. The West German government was pretty sceptical about the Common Market idea, fearing that protectionist arrangements would hamper the global activities of its highly competitive manufacturing industry. Bonn accepted the Treaties of Rome primarily for more abstract political reasons, not because it wanted the Common Market. Barely a decade after the end of the war, this move helped the young West German state to regain international recognition after the horror of the Nazi era. European integration was an end in itself that paradoxically expanded the opportunities open to the still only partially sovereign German state.

The French government did argue for agricultural integration, but the same can be said of the Dutch. While the treaty of 1957 laid out comparatively clear and binding rules for the Common Market, this applied much less to agriculture. In fact, when the treaty was signed it was by no means clear that anything would come of its agricultural component. All in all, France and Germany both played significant roles, but the interests were a great deal too complex to speak of a simple bilateral quid pro quo.

That is even clearer when the role of non-state actors is taken into account.

All six governments ultimately prioritised the broader political picture over economic and technical interests, otherwise they would never have been able to reach agreement. But at the same time the treaties were couched loosely enough to allow each of the six to find aspects that offered economic reward. This was a historically unique period of economic growth, the postwar boom or *'trente glorieuses'*. Finally emerging from an era of death and destruction, western European societies now brimmed with optimism. The future seemed bright and promising: rational, well-planned policies could make a difference. This cultural climate expanded decision makers' political leeway, while the Cold War generated pressure to find solutions. The thaw following Stalin's death in 1953 was brief; the crushing of the Hungarian uprising in 1956 dispelled any doubts about the limits of liberalisation in the Eastern Bloc. That welded the West even closer together. Another factor driving in the same direction was the failure of existing western European organisations to fulfil the expectations placed on them. The Council of Europe, for instance, remained too technical and marginal to tackle the pressing issues of the time. At a deeper level, European power projection was fading. In late 1956 British, French, and Israeli forces invaded Egypt, seeking to regain control of the Suez Canal and remove Egypt's independent-minded President Gamal Abdel Nasser. The operation was opposed by Washington and ended in humiliation for the European powers. After the shock of the Suez Crisis the French and British elites could no longer deny that

2.1 A New Start

their empires were slipping away. In such uncertain times it was obvious for Europe to close ranks.

The role of Washington's goodwill and support should not be forgotten either. Its security umbrella created a central precondition for European integration, and the United States explicitly encouraged the efforts to establish the two Communities, as it had already with the ECSC and the ill-fated EDC. Sometimes, US representatives pushed too hard. In December 1953, as French resistance to the EDC project grew in advance of the parliamentary vote, Secretary of State John Foster Dulles threatened an 'agonising reappraisal' of US policy towards western Europe.[4] But this pressure, bordering on open blackmail, had the opposite effect. It was one of the reasons why the French National Assembly blew the project out of the water the following summer. Subsequently the United States learned to be more discreet and subtle in its support for European integration.

It did so despite the potential economic disadvantages for the United States posed by the EEC and Euratom. Dulles in particular underlined the primacy of the political, treating European integration as a means to shape a new entity in America's image and within the Atlantic partnership. Altogether Washington was to exert fundamental influence on the history of European integration for decades to come.

All this played out largely behind closed doors (Figure 2.3). While parliamentary ratification was quick and easy in all six member states, most people knew little

---

[4] 'Statement by the Secretary of State to the North Atlantic Council', 14 December 1953, in *Foreign Relations of the United States, 1952–1954, Western European Security*, vol. V, part 1 (Washington, DC: U.S. Government Printing Office, 1983), p. 463.

2 Under the Radar, 1950–1969

FIGURE 2.3 National representatives signing the Treaties of Rome in the Palazzo dei Conservatori in Rome, 25 March 1957. First on the left (front row) is Paul-Henri Spaak, who played a key role in the negotiations. Credit: Getty Images 89866232.

about the treaties and cared less. In January 1957 an opinion poll in West Germany found that 49 per cent had heard of the terms 'Common Market' and 'European Economic Community', but only 17 per cent knew what they meant. By January 1958 the figures had risen slightly, to 56 and 21 per cent, although only 28 per cent were sure that the treaty had already been signed.[5] West Germany was not the only country with such poor figures. In France in May 1957 only 35 per cent knew that their own country was involved in Euratom, which their government considered a French prestige project. The historic significance of the treaties was by no means clear to most people in 1957.[6]

---

[5] Elisabeth Noelle and Erich Peter Neumann (eds.), *Jahrbuch der öffentlichen Meinung 1958–1964* (Allensbach: Verlag für Demoskopie, 1965), pp. 542–543.

[6] Horst Möller and Klaus Hildebrand (eds.), *Bundesrepublik Deutschland und Frankreich: Dokumente 1949–1963*, vol. 4 (Munich: K. G. Saur, 1999), p. 57.

2.1 A New Start

That remained the case in the coming years. In 1962, for example, a survey found that most people approved of 'the idea of European integration' but lacked even the most basic knowledge. In Italy 77 per cent were unable to name anything specific that was positive about the EEC and all 100 per cent of survey respondents were unable to name anything negative. For Belgium, France, and West Germany the figures were 59/97, 60/93, and 60/84 per cent.[7] There was little improvement by the end of the decade: 87 per cent of respondents in the six member states approved in some form or other of the integration process, 27 per cent 'strongly' – but only 36 per cent could correctly name the six member states.[8] So support for the Europe of the EEC did not necessarily imply knowledge of even the most basic facts.

Approval was often lip service; the integration process was supported as long as it remained abstract and had little effect on everyday life. As soon as it became concrete the figures fell noticeably. Nothing illustrates this more clearly than opinion polls in the Netherlands, France, the United Kingdom, and West Germany in the early 1960s, which showed large majorities in favour of European integration. But when participants were asked about specific measures the approval rates often dropped by 10 to 20 percentage points.[9] Active support for European integration would have

---

[7] Historical Archives of the European Union, CEAB2/2174, Gallup International, L'opinion publique et l'Europe des six, Paris 1962, quote p. 4.
[8] Commission des Communautés Européennes, *Les Européens et l'unification de l'Europe* (Brussels: European Commission, 1972), pp. 55, 201.
[9] Ronald Inglehart, 'An End to European Integration?', *American Political Science Review* 61 (1967), pp. 91–105.

looked different. Here we already see an inkling of problems that would later truly plague the EU.

2.2 A Market with Appendages

Given this complicated back story, the developments of the subsequent decade appear all the more astonishing. This applies first and foremost to the Common Market, which increasingly pulled ahead of the other two Communities to establish itself as the centre of gravity of European integration. The EEC treaty foresaw the market being realised in three transitional phases. The point was to dismantle most tariff barriers and import/export quotas between member states while leaving non-tariff trade barriers largely untouched. There was also a common external trade policy and moves to enable free movement of goods, persons, services, and capital. All these initiatives were designed to overcome long-established restrictions within Europe.

The treaty's ambitious goals were achieved by July 1968, eighteen months ahead of schedule. A few years earlier Walter Hallstein, the EEC Commission's confident first president, had stressed that the logic behind his Community 'clearly bears some resemblance to that of a federation of states'.[10] That was naturally miles ahead of what had actually been achieved and provides a sense of the enormous dynamism of integration and the high hopes that some of those involved associated with the fledgling institutions.

These trends were favoured by the circumstances. The EEC's dismantling of internal barriers and construction

---

[10] Walter Hallstein, *United Europe: Challenge and Opportunity* (Cambridge, MA: Harvard University Press, 1962), p. 28.

of joint rules for external trade coincided with a phase of enormous economic growth that lent additional legitimacy to integration, especially where the political consensus in the member states at that time rested on a US-inspired 'politics of productivity'.[11] Economic recovery and efficiency were the priorities; growth would iron out any political conflicts of goals. Despite the contemporaneous obsession with prosperity, it is impossible to quantify the precise economic effects of the market regulations, especially when other organisations like the UNECE and the OEEC (OECD from 1961) were also working to ease trade. But it is certainly fair to assert that the EEC made a small but tangible contribution to increasing prosperity during those boom years. The best available figures place the growth effect attributable to European integration at between 0.5 and 0.6 per cent per annum.[12]

Another sphere in which the EEC made notable progress was the establishment of a common competition policy, including a prohibition on abuse of market dominance and a ban on cartels. The economies of the member states

---

[11] Charles S. Maier, 'Between Taylorism and Technocracy: European Ideologies and the Vision of Industrial Productivity in the 1920s', *Journal of Contemporary History* 5 (1970), pp. 27–61.

[12] See, most importantly, Barry Eichengreen and Andrea Boltho, 'The Economic Impact of European Integration', in Stephen Broadberry and Kevin H. O'Rourke (eds.), *The Cambridge Economic History of Modern Europe*, vol. 2: *1870 to the Present* (Cambridge: Cambridge University Press, 2010), pp. 267–295, here p. 282; see also Barry Eichengreen, *The European Economy since 1945: Coordinated Capitalism and Beyond* (Princeton: Princeton University Press, 2007), p. 181; Béla Balassa, 'Trade Creation and Diversion in the European Common Market: An Appraisal of the Evidence', in Béla Balassa (ed.), *European Economic Integration* (Amsterdam: North-Holland Publishing Company, 1975), pp. 79–118.

were exposing themselves to sharper competition – but within a controlled framework. The calculation, in particular of the French and Italian governments, was that a limited opening would spur modernisation of the less competitive sectors of their economies. And throughout the process, Europe has frequently served as a tool for pushing through unpopular domestic reforms.

The project that consumed the greatest political, administrative, and financial resources turned out to be the Common Agricultural Policy (CAP). In this field, the transitional phase was completed even before July 1968. It is remarkable that agreement was reached at all in this notoriously difficult sector. An earlier attempt to create a 'green Europe' in the early 1950s had been blocked by a powerful transnational alliance of agricultural lobbies. Great credit must go to the responsible EEC Commissioner, the Dutchman Sicco Mansholt, who outplayed the opposition in the 1960s by dividing the negotiations into a multitude of minor individual decisions. The task was still enormous. Even more than in the Common Market for industrial goods, the CAP went beyond 'negative' integration (in the value-neutral sense of dismantling obstacles such as tariffs) and moved into the territory of 'positive' integration. In concrete terms this meant in the first place common producer prices for all the main agricultural products, with the CAP intervening deeply in the member states' markets. The roots of this highly interventionist approach go back a long way, originating in the deep transformation crisis that had affected the sector since the 1870s. Since then, agricultural incomes had consistently lagged behind the rest of the economy, and nation states had created subsidy schemes to boost production. This approach was now lifted to the

2.2 A Market with Appendages

European level. But the CAP was not just about helping a sector in crisis. The need to secure food supplies represented a second reason to proactively reshape the sector. This was no trivial matter in a continent with recent memories of wartime shortages and a threatening global situation.

For many policymakers in Brussels the CAP was thus a success story. But it also quickly gained notoriety for its aberrations, as interventionism encouraged massive protectionism. It granted producers significant incentives to increase production, for which they received a kind of sales guarantee. This approach built on existing interventionist agricultural policies in the member states, but its impact was enormously boosted by its Europeanisation. The political elites also faced great pressure from the sector's powerful and well-connected lobbies, whose doubts had to be assuaged with costly concessions. Bonn blew hot and cold and transpired to be the most troublesome negotiating partner. Ultimately, however, even the West Germans signed up to the CAP after dramatic negotiations sometimes dragging on for weeks. And in the end, ironically, Bonn bore most of the responsibility for prices being set high to incentivise production and maximise output.

The upshot was massive overproduction, subsidised through taxation and destroyed (at further expense) or sold at a loss outside the Community. As well as driving up consumer prices, this drew justified criticism from the EEC's global trading partners. The CAP quickly became synonymous with senseless overproduction, with 'butter mountains' and 'wine lakes' entering everyday language, not to speak of the associated environmental harm. These latter problems only started to be addressed seriously in the 1990s and 2000s.

The positive side of the CAP should not be written out of history, however. The massive transformation of European agriculture in the first half of the twentieth century – from the lifeworld of the majority into a small but highly efficient economic sector – generated political extremism and undermined democracy. Intra-European transfer now cushioned the process. Farmers still protested, but radicalisation was kept in check. In that sense the CAP represented a covert form of European social policy. While the EEC lacked the powers to prevent war, it did help to stabilise the social fabric of its states: the welfare gains of integration contributed to social peace.

Whatever one thought about the CAP, its complexity, its burgeoning bureaucracy, and its controversial nature made this agricultural afterthought into the beating green heart of the Community. In the Commission, the directorate-general (DG) in charge of the CAP was by far the largest, and quickly acquired a reputation as the 'glamour DG'.[13] As the first major common policy it left a huge mark on the entire integration process during the EEC's first decade and well beyond.

The history of the CAP, a rather vague and ancillary project in the EEC treaty and soon the Community's real centre of gravity, also holds another lesson. There was no fixed system or logic defining what the EEC should concentrate on. Unlike the ECSC treaty, which laid out the rules in great detail, the EEC treaty provided extensive powers in broad areas like agricultural policy. Vaguely defined legal provisions opened up new

---

[13] Hans J. Michelmann, *Organisational Effectiveness in a Multinational Bureaucracy* (Farnborough: Saxon House, 1978), p. 162.

2.2 A Market with Appendages

possibilities but also increased the risk of failure. That for example was the fate of the transport policy, which was also mentioned in the treaty but never took off during the Cold War. The same can be said of the idea of a proactive social policy, excepting the special case of the CAP. The key to success lay in what the participating governments and other actors were able to agree in negotiations, which sometimes only became apparent during the implementation process.

Something else was perhaps more important. The photograph of the EEC Commission in 1959 (Figure 2.4)

FIGURE 2.4 EEC Commission meeting, 1959. Credit: European Communities, 1959, ID: P-008949/00-14.

might look boring at first glance: roughly a dozen middle-aged men in suits gathered around a table covered with papers, along with a woman with a fashionable hairstyle, seen only from behind. The composition certainly captures the gendered order of European policy-making at the time. The woman is Renée van Hoof, an interpreter who later became the first woman to lead a directorate-general at the Commission. She was also instrumental in establishing the EC's interpreting service, which became the world's largest. Van Hoof had been born into a German middle-class family of Jewish origin and had survived the Holocaust in hiding in Belgium. Right opposite her sat the bespectacled Commission President Walter Hallstein. Also German, Hallstein had been an artillery officer in the Wehrmacht and was now a Christian democrat. The man on van Hoof's right was Commissioner Lambert Schaus from Luxembourg. As a local councillor, he had refused to cooperate with the Germans during the occupation. In 1941 he had been detained by the Gestapo and deported to Germany as a slave labourer. To his right was Robert Marjolin from France. During the war he had been an economic adviser to the French government in exile and undertook several secret missions in Nazi-occupied Europe. On the opposite side of the table, with the dark-framed glasses, was Belgian Jean Rey, a former reserve officer who had spent most of the war as a German prisoner of war. Fourteen years after these formative experiences, they were sat around a table working hard to build a better and united Europe. Instead of hard-nosed pursuit of specific interests, they focused on compromise and reconciliation. Instead of hypertrophied nationalism, they sought close international cooperation. Some of them were even looking towards a European federal state.

That approach, based on intense cooperation between the participating states, soon spread far and wide. European issues were not the sole concern of heads of state and government and their ministers; in the member states hundreds and soon thousands of officials and politicians in fields including foreign affairs, economics, agriculture, and finance were in increasingly close contact with colleagues from other member states, often over significant periods. The same applies to lobbyists, journalists, and other members of a growing transnational elite. The culture of compromise formed the basis for substantive results. Conversely, every political result strengthened the shared culture. This interplay fundamentally transformed the character of politics. Luuk van Middelaar pithily summed up the effects of this web of connections: the 'de-dramatisation' of European politics was a merit of the Community that cannot be overstated.[14] In this respect, the photograph described above was indeed typical for European integration – precisely in its lack of drama.

The phenomenon of the full potential of the EEC only unfolding in the course of implementation is also reflected in another dimension, the role of law. The reason for this was by no means solely the treaty itself and its 248 articles. Instead, the practice of market integration unleashed legal dynamics that would radically reshape the Community in the medium term. Decisions

---

[14] Luuk van Middelaar, *The Passage to Europe: How a Continent Became a Union* (New Haven, CT: Yale University Press, 2013), p. 303.

of the European Court of Justice (ECJ) played a central role in catapulting the EEC well beyond the framework laid out in its treaty. It was not clear from the outset that European law could and would supersede national law; the treaties permitted both interpretations. The turning point was the van Gend en Loos case in 1963, where the court first stepped beyond the traditional bounds of international law. A year later, the Costa/ENEL case confirmed the primacy of Community law over national law. At the time, however, the full implications of these two rulings were not yet apparent. It was to be a decade before they would begin initiating the move towards a legal order with constitutional components.

The EEC also proved highly dynamic in relation to enlargement. In 1960 the British government initiated – in direct competition to the six – a seven-member organisation in the sphere of economic and especially trade policy. This was the European Free Trade Association (EFTA) comprising Austria, Denmark, Norway, Portugal, Sweden, Switzerland, and the United Kingdom. The creation of the EEC and EFTA represented a schism (Map 2.1). Now western Europe was divided into two trade blocs – actually three, given that some countries remained outside of both. Alongside the 'inner six' and the 'outer seven', the 'forgotten five', as they were sometimes called, cooperated with the other thirteen under the loose umbrella of the OEEC. But the very next year the British changed their minds and applied to join the EEC – which was already clearly the more dynamic platform. An accession request from their leading rival was naturally a feather in the cap of the six. Denmark, Ireland, and Norway, which were economically dependent on the United Kingdom, also

2.2 A Market with Appendages

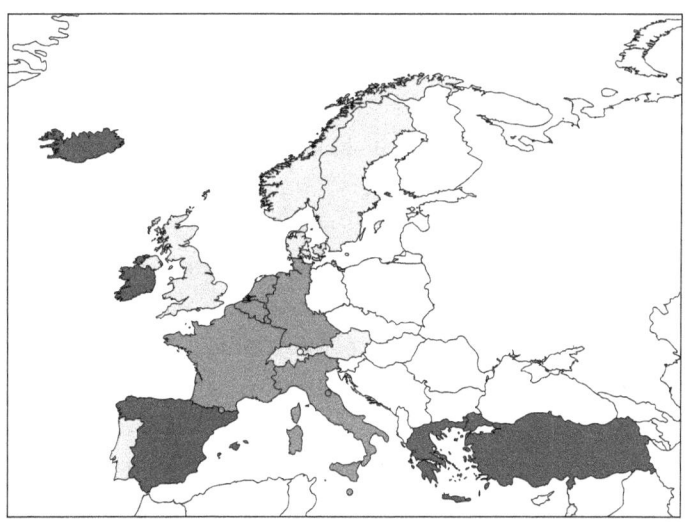

Key:
Medium grey: EEC
Light grey: EFTA
All three colours: OEEC

MAP 2.1 EEC, EFTA, and OEEC member states, 1960.

submitted membership applications together with the British in 1961 and 1967. French President Charles de Gaulle vetoed the British applications on both occasions, fearing that the United Kingdom's accession would change the character of the Community forever. Nonetheless, the Community's attraction remained undimmed and British interest persisted.

During this period the Community also developed its external voice and broadened its visibility. Even if economic policy remained a national responsibility and was shaped by different underlying ideas, the EEC now frequently spoke with a single voice in trade negotiations. This was very apparent in the context of the international General Agreement on Tariffs and Trade (GATT) talks, above all during the Kennedy Round of 1964 to 1967, which instituted massive tariff reductions especially for manufactured goods. The individual member states could never have asserted their interests as well as they did in concert under the EC's Commissioner for External Relations, the Belgian Jean Rey.

The EC also operated as one in another relevant sphere, relations with (former) colonies. In the mid-1950s many Europeans still believed that colonialism had a future and that Africa in particular could be attached to an integrating Europe, in a late-colonial fantasy sometimes referred to as 'Eurafrica'. European integration was not something that started after the end of empire; it was an effort to rescue the imperial nation state in Europe. World history had different plans, however. Decolonialisation really took off in the early 1960s, as a growing number of states cast off the chains of empire. So the relevant provisions of the EEC treaty were soon put to the test. The 1963 Yaoundé Agreement largely confirmed the Community's existing association policy, which granted the former colonies privileged access to EEC markets but cemented the structural supremacy of Europe's industrialised economies. Thus the association policy transitioned from an instrument of late colonialism into a compass for navigating the turbulence of decolonialisation. For example, the EEC's investment fund supported local industries in Africa but made absolutely sure that this did not generate unwanted competition for Europe's own producers. Yaoundé was also significant as the point where the EEC institutionalised its role as a development actor in its own right, even if the nation states were always to remain more significant in this connection.

2.2 A Market with Appendages

The Merger Treaty of 1965 made the three Communities more compact and somewhat less mystifying. It brought them closer without fusing them entirely. This is the point where the term 'European Communities' gained currency, soon referred to in the singular as the European Community. The entity as a whole was now called the EC, but increasingly this was taken to refer principally to the EEC as the most dynamic and visible element.

While the EEC made rapid progress in market integration, agricultural policy, enlargement, and external relations, the same cannot be said for other questions. After winning independence from France in a brutal and bloody war, Algeria left the Community – of which it had de facto been a part in most respects – in 1962. This little-known episode reveals clear early counter-currents to the apparently dominant enlargement narrative.

Yet another group of problems illustrates the importance of implementing treaty decisions and the complexity of real integration. The Treaties of Rome were less supranational than the ECSC and granted more power to the respective Councils of Ministers, as the representation of the member states. But the EEC treaty foresaw a successive expansion of majority voting during the transitional phase. Majority voting meant that a country could be outvoted, even on important matters. The original treaty had laid out a firm timeline for the Community to progress inexorably towards a supranational system. It was on the road to the 'ever closer union' mentioned in the preamble to the EEC treaty.[15]

---

[15] For an English version of the original treaty, see Appendix A in Barnett Cocks, *The European Parliament: Structure, Procedure and Practice* (London: Her Majesty's Stationary Office, 1973), quote p. 153.

France called a halt in the mid-1960s, and the EC remained a more hybrid creature than originally envisaged. On 1 July 1965 Charles de Gaulle's Foreign Minister Maurice Couve de Murville announced the French government's decision to vacate its seat in the Council of Ministers until certain problems it regarded as central had been resolved. This represented the culmination of a longer trend in which de Gaulle pulled no punches in asserting his demands, especially in relation to the CAP. The 'empty chair crisis' in summer 1965 revolved around the planned transition to majority voting; there were also demands relating to agricultural policy and criticisms of the expansive policy of the European Commission under President Hallstein. After the defence community debacle of 1954 this was the next existential test for the Community. After six months of intense negotiations the member states settled on the Luxembourg Compromise at the end of January 1966: they agreed to disagree. The informal arrangement going forward was that no member state could be outvoted where 'vital interests' were involved.[16] Little changed in practice – except the future. The incremental transition to supranationality was truncated and the intergovernmental principle reinforced. This loss of utopia, which also significantly clipped the powers of the European Commission, represented an important turning point in the European integration process.

[16] Document 38: 'The Luxembourg Agreement: Agreement on Decision-Making Reached at the Extraordinary Session of the EEC Council on 28 and 29 January 1966', in A. G. Harryvan and Jan van der Harst (eds.), *Documents on European Union* (Houndmills: Macmillan, 1997), pp. 151–152.

2.2 A Market with Appendages

De Gaulle left his mark more broadly during this phase, which coincided largely with his time as French president from 1959 to 1969. Even before the empty chair crisis he had been working to push the Community towards intergovernmentalism, striving for a Europe of sovereign states under French leadership and only loosely tied to the United States. That does not mean that de Gaulle was against Europe, but he wanted a different Europe than the one for which the EC stood. The Fouchet Plans presented by his government in 1961 and 1962 would have increased political, cultural, and military integration – with a weaker Commission and fewer supranational components. The proposal would have threatened the existing Communities and was roundly rebuffed by the other member states. In response de Gaulle did a U-turn and sought at least closer cooperation with Bonn. The Elysée Treaty of 1963 deepened the bilateral relationship, but the German Bundestag insisted on a pro-American preamble – torpedoing de Gaulle's underlying plan to tie West Germany closer to France and relativise the role of European integration and the transatlantic relationship.

All eyes were thus on the EEC. But what happened to the other organisation set up under the Treaties of Rome? Euratom turned out to be less dynamic than Monnet and others had hoped. France went its own way in civil use of nuclear energy and efforts to bundle nuclear research were unsuccessful. The Merger Treaty in 1965 revised Euratom's remit; the organisation increasingly developed into a precursor of the Community's research policy and a platform for transatlantic debates about technological cooperation. A far cry from the grand schemes of the 1950s, but a typical trajectory for European

2 Under the Radar, 1950–1969

integration: after failing to achieve its original goal, the organisation simply found itself a new purpose.

Overall, these first two decades of EC-style European integration were definitely a mixed bag. Great expectations were dashed, many projects were abandoned unfinished, and there were serious disagreements over the direction of travel. The European Community was a latecomer in an already densely populated field of international organisation: the UNECE, Council of Europe, WEU, and OEEC to name only the most prominent. There was no sense that it would one day occupy the dominant position. Crises and restarts characterised the process, along with the external pressures of the Cold War and support from the United States. But it would be wrong to assume that the nations of western Europe were choosing primarily between national sovereignty and EC-style integration. There were also many other international forums and proposals, even if the EC did always see itself as *the* alternative to nation-centred politics. In another respect this was all not such a new start, as the process certainly built on interwar developments in terms of ideas and personalities. For example, Jean Monnet earned his spurs in the Allied Maritime Transport Council during the First World War, later in the League of Nations; he carried much of that experience into the post-war debates. These aspects remained firmly in the shadows, however, while the protagonists of European integration sought to present it as a radical break with the past.

At the beginning of the 1960s it was by no means clear that the geographically limited project of the six would escape the fate of so many other international

2.2 A Market with Appendages

organisations – starting with a bang but quickly reduced to technical matters with little or no influence on international cooperation, especially monetary matters. In the meantime, as we know, the organisation has exponentially expanded its functions and – despite setbacks – progressed further than many would have thought possible. But it did not yet, at this point, possess real systemic relevance for the member states' economies, still less their societies. Its powers were too weak for that.

The EC succeeded in establishing a certain division of labour in the field of international cooperation. Left to its own devices it would have been overwhelmed by the enormous challenges of the period. It included some of Europe's most powerful states, all keeping multiple irons in the fire: NATO was responsible for security, the Council of Europe for human rights, and the Bretton Woods organisations – the International Monetary Fund and the World Bank – for the transatlantic economic framework. The EC had space to grow at its own pace, cocooned by other organisations in a finely honed division of labour. It certainly helped that few of these organisations were tied to a specific policy area, and reasons of institutional self-preservation motivated many to expand and deepen their activities.

For the time being the EC was more aspiration and assertion than facts on the ground. In these early years the EC was one rather small club among many, with only relative differences to other international organisations in western Europe. It certainly possessed great potential on account of the singular status of the Franco-German relationship, its supranational components, and other factors to which we will come, but this was not obvious at the time. All this underlines the unlikely nature of its rise to become – as the EU – the dominant format of cooperation and integration in Europe.

Questions

1. What were the main motives for European integration during this period? Make your case referring to a concrete example.
2. The EEC turned out to be the most dynamic of the three Communities. Why? Was that clear from the beginning? Discuss.
3. Was European integration a result of the end of European empires?

3
Transformation by Stealth, 1969–1992

3.1 Crisis? What Crisis?

It was not until the last two decades of the Cold War that the EC gradually gelled into a systemically relevant force. Only now does the story leading to its contemporary predominance really begin. To put it another way: it is only because the Community succeeded in growing well beyond its original meaning – as happened in the 1970s and 1980s – that it today decides the fate of entire economies and countries.

This phase of European integration began auspiciously, with few signs that the European project would soon be bogged down in problems – or that it would become so important in the long run. In early December 1969 the heads of state and government of the six member states met in The Hague to thrash out the next steps. Changes in leadership played a role. The long era of de Gaulle ended in April 1969, and with it his intransigence and his veto on British membership. His successor Georges Pompidou, although also a Gaullist, wanted a fresh start: it was he who called the meeting in The Hague. Another propitious sign came from West Germany, where Willy Brandt became Chancellor just six weeks before the summit. Pompidou (born 1911) was twenty-one years younger than de Gaulle; Brandt (born 1913) was nine and sixteen years younger than his two immediate predecessors – and almost thirty-eight years younger

3 Transformation by Stealth, 1969–1992

than Konrad Adenauer, who had led Germany from 1949 to 1963. A new generation had taken the reins in the two largest member states and regarded this as an opportunity to breathe new life into the European project.

The six leaders at The Hague agreed far-reaching decisions on the future development of the EC, many of which were implemented within a few years. Firstly, less than six months after the summit it was decided to grant the EC its own source of income, principally drawn from tariffs and CAP revenues. This placed the Community on a secure long-term footing. Most importantly, it safeguarded the Common Agricultural Policy, for which Paris in particular had long been pressing. These revenues, which supplemented the member states' budget contributions, also noticeably expanded the Community's room for manoeuvre. Secondly, the six defined several policy areas where they wanted to deepen integration, above all in connection with economic and monetary union, foreign policy cooperation, and research and technology cooperation. While all this sounded impressive, it was as yet little more than a declaration of intent. Thirdly, the Hague summit cleared the path to the first round of widening (enlargement): on 1 January 1973 the United Kingdom, the Republic of Ireland, and the Kingdom of Denmark joined the EC. Norway pulled out at the last minute, and the British accession had to be confirmed in a referendum just two years later. Despite these caveats the accession of new member states confirmed the Community's attractiveness and underlined its importance. Completion (of the Common Market and the CAP), deepening (through new policy areas), and widening: the EC was now making progress in all three areas Pompidou had floated when he called the summit.

3.1 Crisis? What Crisis?

In many ways the Hague summit represented the kind of compromise that was typical of European politics. Bonn had pushed particularly hard to reopen the door for enlargement negotiations, while Paris insisted on finalising the CAP and its finances. Both sides – and to a large extent also the other four participating governments – got what they wanted but also had bitter pills to swallow. The CAP offers an obvious example. West Germany's best-known cartoonist of the time, Hanns Erich Köhler, encapsulated its problems for readers of the *Frankfurter Allgemeine Zeitung* on the second day of the summit (Figure 3.1). He depicted an

2. Dezember 1969   EWG-Gipfel
„Oben vom Butterberg haben wir eine herrliche Aussicht auf den Zuckerkogel, das Getreidemassiv und ganz in weiter Ferne auf England."

FIGURE 3.1 Cartoon 'EEC Summit', Hanns Erich Köhler, 2 December 1969. Credit: Wilhelm Busch – Deutsches Museum für Karikatur und Zeichenkunst.

enthusiastic Pompidou urging an exhausted Brandt to continue a difficult climb: 'When we get to the top of the butter mountain, we'll have a lovely view of the sugarloaf and the grain mountains. And in the far distance we'll just about be able to see England.' As Köhler's cartoon implies, the summit consolidated the CAP's surpluses – which principally benefited French agriculture. While the effects were problematic for taxpayers, consumers, and agricultural producers in third countries, the outcomes of the Hague summit massively strengthened institutional Europe.

The northern enlargement was immensely significant for the history of European integration – and for boosting the institutions. In some respects, it was the most important enlargement of all, in tangible as well as symbolic terms. This holds true even in comparison to 2004, when ten states with 74 million inhabitants joined the EU. The 1973 enlargement involved only three states with 64 million people between them. But in relative terms it expanded the Community's population by 33 per cent, compared to 20 per cent in 2004. In terms of GDP too, the relative increase in 1973 was significantly greater than in 2004. This substantially expanded market stepped up the Community's growth potential.[1] From a club with a handful of members, the EC was transformed into an association representing most of western Europe, with commensurate economic clout.

That sounds like a lot but soon turned out to be too little. For the circumstances within which the EC was operating

---

[1] For further details on these figures, see Alain Monnier, 'The European Union at the Time of Enlargement', *Population (English Edition)* 59 (2004), pp. 315–336.

were about to change dramatically. Tying up loose ends was no longer enough. Too many new issues were jostling for attention. Important sections of the cocoon that had cloaked and stabilised the EC broke away in the early 1970s. This was most obvious in the economic sphere. The historically unprecedented post-war boom that oiled the wheels of the early integration process came to a juddering halt in the early 1970s. Now the EC faced the multiple challenges of 'stagflation', with economic stagnation, high inflation, rising unemployment, and growing state debt. New protest movements drove change in the social and political spheres and anti-capitalist ideas proliferated. This was certainly a challenging time for the elite-driven EC and its capitalist DNA.

The end of the boom also blew holes in the global structures from which the EC had hitherto profited. This applies in particular to the Bretton Woods system as an international monetary order with fixed exchange rate bands anchored by the US dollar. Without that certainty, western Europe had to rethink its monetary order. As well as deepening the economic crisis, the oil price shocks of 1973 and 1979/80 revealed how dependent western Europe had become on the black gold and its Middle Eastern suppliers. Oil shortages also drew attention to the finite nature of natural resources. The environmental 'limits to growth' were laid out in 1972 in a widely noted study by the Club of Rome,[2] and the ecological problems associated with the fossil age were now subject to

---

[2] Donella H. Meadows et al., *The Limits to Growth: A Report for the Club of Rome's Project on the Predicament of Mankind* (New York: Universe Books, 1972).

3 Transformation by Stealth, 1969–1992

intense public discussion. Across the board a new wave of globalisation exposed the economies of western Europe to growing pressure of competition. Old certainties vanished in a flash.

In the sphere of security too, the rigid coordinates of the Cold War were giving way to a new and less predictable world. Dangerous regional conflicts flared up – such as the Yom Kippur War of 1973 between Israel and its Arab neighbours – while paradoxically tensions relaxed between the superpowers. This was especially clear in 1973, when the Conference on Security and Cooperation in Europe (CSCE) convened after a series of preparatory meetings. Western Europe had to adopt a position on the ensuing East–West meetings – the Helsinki Process – which involved almost all the states of Europe. And even more importantly, however much they welcomed détente, the process also raised unsettling questions over Washington's security guarantee. The problem became all the more pressing as the transatlantic relationship deteriorated visibly during the presidency of Richard Nixon. Not least on account of its own problems, the United States no longer supported the integration process as generously as it had since the late 1940s. All these shifts placed the EC under pressure, and it was unclear whether it would be part of the problem or the solution.

The European Community responded in a variety of ways to these challenges. New institutions and instruments were introduced to improve the organisation's effectiveness. Two of the most important initiatives arose without a clear basis in the treaties: the European Political Cooperation (EPC) and the European Council both emerged informally outside the EC's *acquis communautaire*, the legal rights and obligations of its members. This was a stunning development, given the EC's ethos of legal formalism. It reflected the member states' growing sense that the economic crisis had become too big to ignore and that the EC was the key institutional format for addressing it at the European level. Despite the lack of a formal seal, the member states were thus seeking to lend the Community greater impact and new significance.

The EC states founded the European Political Cooperation in 1970 to institutionalise their foreign policy cooperation. The EPC was a purely intergovernmental structure for foreign policy consultations, for which the EC had hitherto lacked any forum. In the EPC the EC states worked to find common ground in order to expand their influence on global politics. This functioned surprisingly well in the Helsinki Process, where the Community frequently spoke with a single voice on crucial Cold War matters, but much less so on practically every other issue in the field of global affairs. The member states had created a new institutional format, but its precise import and impact remained rather unclear.

During this same period the exception of the Hague Summit became the rule: from the mid-1970s the EC heads of state and government met regularly for European summits. Where the heads of state and government had previously come together only sporadically and mostly for ceremonial occasions, they now convened formally as the 'European Council' (not to be confused with the Council of Europe, which remained a separate organisation). EC policy would no longer be left to the respective Council of Ministers formats. The European Council

3 Transformation by Stealth, 1969-1992

weakened the supranational aspect and strengthened the intergovernmental principle; now the heads of state and government were held much more directly responsible.

The emergence of the EPC and the European Council reflected an awareness that a world of new challenges had to be addressed with innovative forms of cooperation. The European institutions – within the EC, but also other forums such as the European Council – entered uncharted waters, and while the EPC chalked up successes in the CSCE its statements on other issues such as the Middle East conflict went unheeded. At the same time security proper remained outside the EC framework, as the preserve of NATO and the nation states, thus placing clear limits on the Community's new engagement. In a similar vein, the work of the European Council was laborious: its everyday efforts often appeared inadequate. Putting national leaders visibly in charge of European integration raised the stakes; it produced great expectations and often enough deep disappointments.

In 1979, the European project's institutional framework underwent an important development in a different direction: the first direct elections to the European Parliament (EP) (whose members had previously been delegated by the parliaments of the member states). This change gave MEPs a stronger mandate and reflected the institution's great desire to participate in the political process. The first directly elected European Parliament chose Simone Veil as its president (Figure 3.2); as a prominent French politician, a Holocaust survivor, and the first woman to fill that position, she personified the parliament's determination to make its mark. In 1979, with Veil at the helm, the European Parliament rejected

3.1 Crisis? What Crisis?

FIGURE 3.2 Simone Veil (1927–2017), president of the first directly elected European Parliament, at her inaugural speech, 17 July 1979.

the EC's budget, utilising for the first time rights granted in 1970 and 1975. French Prime Minister Raymond Barre, in whose cabinet Veil had served just a few months earlier, called her some twenty times to change her mind, but to no avail. The European Parliament insisted on amendments before it would pass the budget.

Veil's role invites a brief discussion on the role of gender. Only 4 per cent of MEPs between 1952 and 1979 were women (mostly from the United Kingdom and Denmark, which only joined in 1973), making Veil's appointment as president of the Parliament all the more remarkable. Since the 1980s the EP has become one of the 'most female' parliaments in Europe. For a long time, the proportion of women increased steadily: around 20 per cent in 1989, 30 per cent in 2004, and 40 per cent in the 2019 elections; in 2024, the figure fell very slightly to 39 per cent. The EP also became more diverse in other

3 Transformation by Stealth, 1969–1992

respects over the course of the decades. The other EU institutions lagged behind. The first female commissioners were not appointed until 1989 (Vasso Papandreou from Greece and Christine Scrivener from France). Only in 1999 did Fidelma Macken from Ireland become the first female judge at the ECJ. And it was not until 2019 that Ursula von der Leyen became the first woman to head the Commission as President. At the time of writing, no person representing the institutions at the highest level has yet identified their gender as 'diverse'.

The EP's significance in comparison to other parliamentary assemblies at the European level is also revealing. Until 1979 many of its members also attended the parliamentary assemblies of organisations like the Council of Europe or the WEU, thus facilitating exchange and cooperation between the various forums. The direct elections introduced in 1979 made the EC more autonomous, with its parliament distinguishing it from 'normal' international organisations.

Overall, though, the significance of 1979 should not be overestimated – even if politicians at the time felt it was a big deal and most of the literature has echoed their views. The EP had been expanding its role in various directions since the 1960s, and both before and after the introduction of direct elections it had a tendency to declare itself responsible for matters where it actually lacked formal powers. In this sense it has always played a part in enlarging the spectrum of topics covered by the EC. Veil, for instance, stressed the importance of human rights and advocated for political prisoners in Turkey after the military coup in 1980. The EP had few formal powers for such issues – it tried as it could, but its successes remained

3.1 Crisis? What Crisis?

very limited. Its aspirations certainly continued to be much larger than its impact.

In parallel to these institutional developments, the EC expanded into new policy areas in the 1970s. Both processes contradict an interpretation that prevails to this day, that the period was dominated by crisis in the integration process. One reason for that misconception is that many of the new initiatives emerged in small, almost imperceptible steps, rather than the grand fanfare of a major treaty reform. Some of the most important were in fact based only on informal arrangements or had their legal basis outside the EC treaties, despite being intimately bound up with the EC. Also, many did not function especially well in the short and medium term, which reinforced the idea of a Community in crisis.

Monetary policy is a case in point. Cracks were already appearing in the Bretton Woods system at the end of the 1960s, before it imploded at the beginning of the 1970s. The resulting exchange rate volatility was compatible neither with the system of guaranteed agricultural prices that the CAP had created in long and laborious negotiations nor with the hopes that had been placed in the Common Market. Strongly fluctuating exchange rates, often the result of unilateral exchange rate decisions, possessed the potential to kill both the CAP and the Common Market. The first tentative steps towards a western European monetary union made slow progress in the crisis-ridden 1970s; after years of discussion the European Monetary System (EMS) saw the light of day in 1979, not least thanks to the personal intervention of French President Valéry Giscard d'Estaing and German Chancellor Helmut Schmidt at the Copenhagen summit

3 Transformation by Stealth, 1969–1992

in the summer of 1978. The EMS defined bands within which the currencies were permitted to float. Despite its weaknesses, 'the snake' saved the Common Market and blunted the impact of the slump. Formally speaking, the EMS was an agreement between EEC member states and not directly part of the Community; the British initially decided to stay outside and only joined in 1990. The EMS thus emblemises the creative search for new ways to deal with pressing problems. But since it affected a core dimension of national sovereignty, it was no longer possible to bring all member states on board.

Other areas where the EC gradually expanded its influence during this period included research, environmental protection and regional policy. In each case the treaties from the 1950s turned out to be flexible enough to serve as the basis for new projects or to permit innovations to emerge outside their remit. For example, this was a period when the EC forged ahead in science and technology. Euratom had established its place in nuclear research in the 1960s. Now the Community broadened its horizons, though always retaining the focus on applied research. In 1977, for instance, it launched initiatives in the groundbreaking fields of computing and aerospace research. This process was undergirded by a broad public debate about the 'technology gap', the idea of catching up with the United States, as the leader, and staying ahead of newcomer Japan. Without this crisis discourse the member states would never have agreed to give the EC such a free hand in this field. Here, as in other questions, the EC succeeded in making an opportunity out of a crisis.

The EC's expanding activities and policy areas also altered its status in relation to other international

3.1 Crisis? What Crisis?

organisations in western Europe. First, it is notable that the EC – rather than the Council of Europe, the OECD, and other forums – was seen as the most suitable platform to which to attach new policy areas and institutional formats. In a sense the crisis revealed which of the existing organisations the political elites of the member states saw as most useful. That would have been much less likely if the crisis had come a decade earlier, when there would have been more doubts about placing such crucial issues in the hands of a fragile EC. In the end its credentials were boosted especially by the northern enlargement and completion of the Common Market. The 1970s also saw intense conflicts between the different international organisations, for example over who should be responsible for the new field of environmental policy. As well as the EC, the OECD, the Council of Europe, and even NATO staked claims. There was a process of continuous recalibration and redistribution. At this point the EC was certainly not solely responsible for new initiatives in international cooperation. But it was astonishingly often chosen to take the lead.

The various international organisations in western Europe were not only competing; they also cooperated and learned from one another. Time and again the EC adopted solutions that had first been tested elsewhere. Environmental policy is a key example, where it borrowed the OECD's 'polluter pays' principle. But within the Common Market its impact was enormous. The EC had already overtaken the OECD in the sphere of trade policy in the 1960s; now, it began moving into traditional preserves of the Council of Europe such as human rights and representing local and regional governments. Yet

3 Transformation by Stealth, 1969–1992

the member states' governments, businesses, and civil society groups did not regard the EC as the sole alternative to national sovereignty or traditional diplomatic formats and made use of a range of channels and institutions. These included new forums such as the Group of Six, established as an informal high-level gathering of the leaders of France, Italy, the United Kingdom, and West Germany from the EC, plus the United States and Japan. While the G6 gathered the finance ministers and, from 1975, the heads of state or government, the CSCE provided a bridge between East and West. All the same, an initially almost imperceptible trend to prioritise the European Community gradually swelled, especially from the early 1980s. At the symbolic level it increasingly embodied the big idea of European cooperation.

So how was the EC able to grow in so many directions at once? And why was it able to outpace all other international organisations in western Europe to become a powerful actor impacting the fate of societies? Three factors stand out. Firstly, the Customs Union and the Common Market remained the Community's heart, a legacy of the EEC's early years. Economic logic quasi-automatically drew in other policy areas. For example, the establishment of the Common Market had immediate implications in areas as diverse as hygiene standards, consumer protection, vocational training, environmental protection, and social policy. That is not to say that these issues fell automatically under the EC's powers. But there were always groups and institutions pushing in that direction, be they the Commission, the Parliament, the Court of Justice, transnational lobbies, or individual member states. From the 1970s, for example, the EC developed a rudimentary cultural policy of its own. The ECJ played a not insignificant role in this, as it had to clarify the extent to which cultural goods fell under the broader rules of the Common Market. Initially the question was exemptions from the Common Market rules, but this soon segued into small explicitly cultural policy initiatives. This would actually have been the role of UNESCO at the international level, and the Council of Europe in Western Europe. Economic reasoning was normally less contentious than political and cultural arguments when pushing for closer international cooperation – and this is exactly how the EC presented its ideas. This was expedited by the capitalist logic of the Cold War confrontation, under which increasing prosperity was an undisputed goal shared by all.

Secondly, law played a role (Figures 3.3 and 3.4). The gradual emergence of a legal culture of its own, with a strongly binding character from legislation to implementation, gave the Community a tangible advantage over other international organisations. The latter generally depended on the voluntary willingness of their member states to implement broadly couched recommendations in national legislation. Under certain circumstances Community citizens were even entitled to bring their own cases before the ECJ, which was certainly not possible in organisations like the OECD. Moreover, the landmark cases of van Gend en Loos and Costa/ENEL in the 1960s established the principles of direct effect of EU law and its primacy over national law. Through such legal activism the EC acquired much greater legal muscle than any normal international organisation. This approach created an unusual dynamic in the development

3 Transformation by Stealth, 1969–1992

FIGURES 3.3 AND 3.4 The Court of Justice on the Kirchberg plateau in Luxembourg. The first permanent new building was the Palais (top figure), completed in 1972. The court's subsequent expansion required the addition of many new buildings, including the three towers (bottom figure). The original Palais is now fully surrounded by the Anneau. Credit: European Court of Justice.

of Community law and turned out to be one of its most effective tools. For example, the ECJ contributed – far more promiscuously than in the aforementioned example of cultural policy – to expanding the EC's powers, not least through its expansive interpretation of the market-related provisions of the treaties. The direct applicability of Community law, which is independent of and overrides the laws of the member states, turned out to be crucial, and also explains why the EC's trade instruments were a class above those of the GATT.

Thirdly and finally, the EC was able to draw on greater financial resources than the other international organisations, especially after acquiring its own revenues through decisions in 1970 and 1975. The OECD's budget for example covered little more than a secretariat, some statistical research, and a few expert committees. The Council of Europe's situation was comparable. The EC on the other hand operated comparatively independently of its member states, especially given that the Commission and Parliament now had a proper say on how the budget was to be spent. This solution was hard fought but once established it granted the EC possibilities its rivals could only dream of.

Together these three factors helped the EC to grow in importance and elevate itself above the other international organisations in Europe. This process accelerated from the 1970s and even more in the course of the 1980s, but played out in tiny steps and went, at this stage, largely unnoticed. Nevertheless, these three drivers explain why, over time, the EC came to influence the fate of whole societies and why its impact on people's everyday lives only grew. From its start as one international

3 Transformation by Stealth, 1969–1992

organisation among others, the EC grew into a supranational structure with great influence. While it never lived up to the hopes of the European federalists, it was now moving much more in that direction than it had during the 1950s and 1960s.

These developments were overlain – and in the public perception dominated – by other aspects, in particular the battles between national leaders. The early 1980s specifically are described in the history books as the heyday of 'Eurosclerosis', when the intransigence of British Prime Minister Margaret Thatcher in particular plunged the EC into crisis. That is not in itself incorrect, even if criticisms of the size of the British contribution to the EC budget had a real basis in the mismatch between the United Kingdom's political economy when it joined in 1973 and the model the EC had established by that time. Specifically, the EC's budget system disadvantaged a large economy with a comparatively small agricultural sector. Thatcher's pugnacious style – which foregrounded national interests and soon found eager followers in several other capitals – made it all the harder to find compromises (Figures 3.5 and 3.6). But just as de Gaulle in the 1960s recognised what the EC was worth to France and knew the line between harsh words and existential crisis, one must not overlook the complexity of British policy in this period. For example, Thatcher's drive to deepen the Common Market was an objective shared by advocates of the supranational approach. For all the European drama, there was a great deal of nuts and bolts policymaking going on in the background.

Through the early 1980s the greater challenge for the EC lay elsewhere and was easy to overlook: not criticism

3.1 Crisis? What Crisis?

FIGURES 3.5 AND 3.6 British Prime Minister Margaret Thatcher at the 1984 Fontainebleau summit (top figure) where she insisted on a reduction in the British budget contribution. And nine years earlier (bottom figure), supporting the 'Yes' campaign during the 1975 referendum confirming membership of the Community. Together, the two images summarise Thatcher's – and the UK's – ambivalence towards the EC. Credit: Getty Images.

of its nature and direction, but member states turning to other very different instruments to address the immense challenges of the time, especially globalisation. For instance, France's president in the early 1980s, François Mitterrand, experimented with a Keynesian reformism that was orientated primarily on the nation state and foresaw little place for the EC. Others looked to global solutions, including the GATT framework. Only after learning that such alternatives were unable to withstand the pressures of the financial markets and other factors, or failed to achieve the desired effects, did the member states return to the EC fold. This successive falling away of alternatives was another factor that put wind in the EC's sails from the mid-1980s and boosted smaller-scale approaches, for example in the external, environmental, and research policies.

Difficult as they are to quantify, the economic effects of European integration were as complex and multilayered as its role during this period. The western European economies remained mired in crisis long after 1973. Real per capita GDP in the six founding states grew between 1973 and 1992 at only roughly half the rate of the period between 1950 and 1973. In other words, their economies were still expanding, but a great deal more slowly than before. The situation was similar in Denmark and Spain, the decline a great deal more dramatic in Portugal and Greece. The slowing of growth was noticeably smaller only in the United Kingdom and Ireland, where the British economy had already been ailing. So, EC membership did not come with a huge economic boost. In fact, the coincidence of the first enlargement and the massive economic deterioration was unfortunate for the EC, which tended to be blamed for the problems. At the same time, it should be noted that across the EC as a whole the share of economic growth attributable to European integration was roughly the same as in the years pre-1973, standing at roughly 0.5 percentage points per annum. So, while overall growth shrank, the *relative* effect of European integration grew significantly. Without the EC, the collapse after the post-war boom would have been even more devastating. European integration remained in the shadows, but certainly made its effects felt.

3.2 Changes

Change was coming, even if that was not clear at the time. During the mid-1980s hitherto almost imperceptible developments started to coalesce into an identifiable trend. The conflict over the British budget contribution was finally laid to rest at the 1984 Fontainebleau summit, after years of talks. A year later the Frenchman Jacques Delors took over as president of the European Commission and rapidly became one of the central movers and shakers of the integration project. The period from 1984 to 1990 also saw slightly better economic growth, lower inflation, and receding unemployment, which opened up political options. The East–West conflict came to an abrupt end in 1989/90 and suddenly a path to a more peaceful and prosperous future seemed possible.

At the same time, the EC was visibly picking up momentum. If the period since the early 1970s had been the warm-up, the project shifted up a gear in the mid-1980s, entering a phase of fundamental transformation and breaking through to become the leading forum in western Europe. The European Community morphed into a markedly different creature to the classical international organisations, assuming an increasingly hegemonic status vis-à-vis the OECD, the Council of Europe, and others. This was formalised in the Maastricht Treaty of 1992, although developments had been starting to move in this direction for some twenty years, and very visibly over the preceding five. Again, the process was driven by small shifts whose details were followed and understood almost exclusively by experts, rather than high-level summits and grand acts of state.

The Single Market programme now became the centre of gravity. Although trade liberalisation represented the raison d'être of the EEC, it had always remained incomplete and new problems had accumulated. For all their commitments to liberalisation, the member states responded to the economic rollercoaster of the 1970s with protectionism, especially in the form of non-tariff barriers. The incoming Delors Commission in 1985 immediately grasped the nettle to argue in dramatic terms for radical change: 'Europe stands at the crossroads. We either go ahead – with resolution and determination – or we drop back into mediocrity.'[3] The 'Single Market' was to be realised by 1992, its name signalising the step forward from the existing Common Market. A programme of work was quickly rolled out, ultimately culminating in the Single European Act and massively advancing economic deepening.

---

[3] *Completing The Internal Market: White Paper from the Commission to the European Council* (Milan, 28–29 June 1985), COM (85) 310, p. 55.

3.2 Changes

Law played a special role here, as one particular ruling of the ECJ from 1979 now finally began to unfold its enormous potential. *Cassis de Dijon* established the principle of mutual recognition: if a product could be legally circulated in one member state under that country's laws, then the other member states were obliged to permit it in their markets too. That may sound rather technical, and so it was. But it had enormous consequences. National isolation was no longer the legal assumption; it now required special justification. Trade barriers became easier to dismantle, because a detailed regulation no longer had to be adopted unanimously in Brussels. This legal approach was increasingly employed from the mid-1980s and its scope expanded. The point was not deregulation, but a fusion of the legal systems of the EC and its member states in a hitherto unseen form, under the banner of unbureaucratic market opening.

This development was predicated on a changing world. Recession and crisis had discredited national and Keynesian models, as well as the earlier liberal consensus. The zeitgeist was turning to neoliberalism, not only in the United Kingdom, and many now signed up to the credo that expanding trade and sharpening competition would generate long-term economic growth, reduce consumer prices, and create employment. The Commission's leap into deeper integration was supported by multinational businesses, and in terms of governments above all by the British. The economic upturn and the unexpected relaxation of East–West tensions in the second half of the 1980s also played their part, soon to be boosted by the debate around the new buzzword of globalisation.

The central expression and motor of this turn was the Single European Act (SEA), which came into force in 1987. As the EC's first major treaty reform since the Treaties of Rome, it comprised an almost unreadable text that amended the existing EEC treaty without replacing any of its core tenets. The devil was in the detail. Among other things the SEA considerably expanded qualified majority voting on matters relating to the Single Market. Even if many governments were less than enthusiastic, the move relativised the effect of the Luxembourg Compromise and significantly curtailed the member states' sovereignty through a technical tweak that passed with little public discussion. In the area of the Single Market this created a deep and mutual interdependency between member states and the Community. The goals were anything but revolutionary but the means chosen were transformative. And, as before, the economy became the main driver deepening the European project.

As well as the Single Market programme, the SEA integrated into the treaties everything that had emerged in the prior fifteen years fully or partly outside them. This included environmental and monetary policy, research and development, and, in the institutional dimension, the EPC and the European Council. At the institutional level the SEA also strengthened the powers of the European Parliament. In fact, this was the first time that an official EC document called it by this name – hitherto, it had mostly been the members of the 'Parliamentary Assembly' who had spoken of it as a 'parliament'. Altogether the SEA tidied up the EC's institutions, consolidating and ordering the existing, and creating a platform for the next integration steps. Enthused by these successes and determined to realise the Single Market by 1992, many of those involved were gripped by a new round of euphoria. The collapse of state socialism and the end of the Cold War added further momentum to these debates. Many Europeans felt they had reached a critical juncture where fantastic new possibilities were appearing. 'Europe' evoked a bright future of prosperity.

The long-term effects of European integration were to be even more far-reaching, as the EC level became increasingly intertwined with state structures and processes – initially in legal enactment but increasingly also in the administrative sphere. The modern state's administrative structures deeply permeate society. Employing these made the EC increasingly omnipresent. Rather than maintaining a large bureaucracy of its own it utilised those of the member states. The European Community stabilised itself through these processes; in fact, it was this growing entanglement with the member states' administrations that created the European institutions in the form we now know. And that also involved a transformation of the existing state structures.

The legal dimension illustrates very clearly how the process accelerated in the second half of the 1980s: between 1958 and 1987 the average number of new directives and regulations introduced annually was 789. Between 1988 and 1992 it spiked above 1,600, only to fall to around 1,300 in the subsequent five years (Figure 3.7).

What emerged was a post-classical form of sovereignty – states cooperating in a partially supranational framework – which some experts believed presaged a process of constitutionalisation. Or put more simply, 'project Europe' became increasingly central to politics,

FIGURE 3.7 Legal acts adopted by the Council and Commission.

economics, and administration. This was neither just Brussels, nor the sum of the member states, but a fusion between the various levels.

Most people, however, hardly noticed this interweaving with state apparatuses and the economy, largely because the consequences did not yet appear to affect them directly. There was certainly grumbling over changes to the familiar nation state. But ultimately lack of interest prevailed, and there was scant discussion about European identity or the pros and cons of integration. Of course, there were debates in Brussels and elsewhere about the need to give the European project stronger democratic legitimacy. But they made little progress, and most energy was channelled instead into symbolic initiatives such as the European flag (Box 3.1).

The EC acquired growing significance in another dimension too. From the 1970s and particularly during the 1980s it increasingly saw itself as a normative power working to stabilise democracy and rule of law through its enlargement processes. While this played no part in the first accession round (Denmark, Ireland, and the United

3.2 Changes

Box 3.1 A flag for the EU

Today's EU flag, with its circle of twelve golden stars on a blue field, has a rich history. It was first developed for and adopted by the Council of Europe in 1955. The early European Community had no clear symbol of its own; its institutions adopted the Council of Europe's emblem in 1985. The Council of Europe supported this step, since it wanted its symbol to be used across European organisations. That was quite a unique position, and ironically the flag is today associated much more with the EU than with the Council of Europe. The symbol's adoption thus epitomises the EC's rise to become the foremost forum of cooperation in western Europe at that time.

There are different interpretations of the flag's meaning. In the twentieth century several other Western and global organisations also chose blue, which carried less clear political connotations than for instance red. The flag's dark shade of blue is sometimes associated with the Virgin Mary. The Council of Europe itself stated that it symbolised the 'blue sky of the Western world', while the invariable number of twelve stars stood for 'perfection and entirety'. Aesthetically, the flag of Belgian Congo – featuring a yellow star on a blue background – served as a major inspiration. This link to a problematic symbol of late colonialism has been almost entirely forgotten today.

Official use in the EC/EU context has expanded greatly since the 1990s, even if the flag still lacks official status under the formative treaties. Resistance to an EU flag, which is often seen as a state-like symbol, has always been strong, and the same applies to other symbols such as an anthem. The 2004 Constitutional Treaty (see Chapter 4) tried to change that, but its failure during the ratification process also prevented the flag from gaining official status. The current EU treaty – the 2009 Lisbon Treaty – avoids the question of a flag altogether.

Kingdom), the issue arose just a few years later in connection with Greece, Spain, and Portugal. All three had only recently shaken off authoritarian regimes when they applied to join the EC in the mid-1970s. Greece submitted its application in 1975, just a year after the toppling of the military junta. As always, the negotiations concerned economic and security questions. But the EC now styled itself as a community of values for the first time. Greek Prime Minister Konstantinos Karamanlis also underlined consolidating democracy as a central motive for joining. Both sides, the Greeks and the EC, employed this argument to convince opponents of the need for Greece, as a comparatively poor and structurally underdeveloped state, to join the EC. For example, Dutch Prime Minister Joop den Uyl responded to doubts over the economic challenges of the southern enlargement by underlining the immense political significance of the EC supporting the fragile post-dictatorship democracy. Values and norms had never been as central for the EC as in the Greek accession process.

The same can be said of Spain and Portugal, both of which applied to join in 1977. Both governments understood this as confirmation of their successful transition to democracy and as a means of consolidating their stabilisation. The EC now became identified with democracy and human rights because – ambivalences aside – it was applying stricter standards than for example NATO or the OECD. Given that the United States had backed the military junta, the EC appeared an attractive alternative to many Greeks. After promoting democracy and human rights had played such a prominent role in the Greek accession, it was obvious that Spain and Portugal should be enabled to join too, even if their economic difficulties were considerably greater.

All this laid the groundwork for the EC to make such a central contribution to the democratic transition in eastern and central Europe a few years later, when the Iron Curtain was swept away. In the second half of the 1980s the EC intensified its trade relations with the states of the Eastern bloc, culminating in their formal recognition of the EC in 1988–89. Soon thereafter, economic assistance was supplied to former communist states restructuring their economies, for example through the PHARE programme, which was originally created to provide financial aid to Poland and Hungary but also supported state reforms. Such initiatives projected the EC's new role beyond its member states.

Since the 1980s intellectuals from central and eastern Europe like Milan Kundera and Czesław Miłosz had dreamt of their nations 'returning' to 'Europe'. When they spoke of 'central Europe' they were distancing themselves from the Soviet Union, while their thoughts revolved around Europe rather than the West or the international community. At the decisive moment Europe found itself – in the guise of the EC – in possession of the political structures it needed to facilitate such a return and channel it into a viable trajectory. It is often overlooked that this had already occurred in 1990, when German unification brought the territory of the former GDR into the EC. In political and symbolic terms, the EC's involvement was crucial to making German unification acceptable to Germany's European partners. The same can be said of the process of overcoming the Cold War divisions more broadly, which would have been almost unimaginable without the EC's prominent role in southern Europe in the 1970s and 1980s. Again, the EC was energised by working to stabilise countries requesting membership. All these developments enormously boosted the role of the European Community in a way nobody would have thought possible twenty years earlier.

Existing ties were also being realigned from the mid-1980s. Questions of democracy and human rights originally played no role in the earlier association agreements and more generally in relationships with the former colonies. The Yaoundé Convention of 1963 was largely built around the principle of non-intervention in the internal affairs of sovereign states. That slowly began to change with the Lomé Convention of 1975, which deepened and expanded cooperation with the former colonies. Where, as in Idi Amin's Uganda, human rights violations occurred on a scale attracting global criticism, the EC restricted its development aid. In the negotiations for Lomé II the European Commission and the British and Dutch governments in particular pressed for relations to be made strongly conditional on human rights, but this was rejected by the other states. Lomé III in 1984 cautiously mentioned human rights for the first time and the trend continued in the late 1980s. All in all, gradual shifts were occurring. A primarily economic project was developing into an entity that increasingly understood itself as a community of values and sought to project these globally. And while Europeans had spent the first post-war decades focusing on adapting late-colonial relations to a postcolonial age, guided by a mix of economic interests, paternalism, and disinterest in African perspectives, they now gave their project a much more ambitious touch.

Such debates also fed back into the treaties. The preamble to the SEA of 1987 noted the determination of the member states 'to work together to promote democracy',[4] singling out the centrality of the fundamental rights laid out in the European Social Charter, which was drawn up by the Council of Europe in 1961. Although the body of the text did little to breathe life into these worthy ideals, it certainly represented a commitment to demanding democracy and fundamental rights in associated and accession-seeking states – and within the Community itself. For all the nods to the work of the Council of Europe, the document underlined the EC's new ambition to take the lead on values and norms.

The attrition of alternatives – in the sense of other international organisations or nation state-centred politics – was thus a fourth factor explaining the EC's rise to become the leading forum of western European cooperation, alongside its economic DNA, its budget, and its legal muscle.

Having said this, the EC's unprecedented rise was associated with a paradoxical counter-tendency within. Exactly at the moment when the project managed to elevate itself above the largely technical and attain gradually systemic significance, centrifugal tendencies accelerated. While there had always been crises and impasses, a new phenomenon emerged in the 1970s: sometimes member states declined outright to participate in

---

[4] Official Journal of the European Communities, L 169, 'Single European Act', 29 June 1987, p. 2.

particular far-reaching projects. Differentiated integration was the price for the EC's growing predominance, discussed at the time under labels such as 'multi-speed Europe', 'variable geometry', or 'Europe à la carte'. This tendency rose to prominence in the mid-1970s in the discussion about a common monetary policy, which touched on a core area of state sovereignty. When the EMS was established in 1979 certain member states were not (yet) willing to subscribe fully to the project. As already mentioned, the United Kingdom did not join the exchange rate mechanism until 1990 and left again in 1992. And this in turn meant that joining the EMS was not an automatic membership requirement in subsequent enlargement rounds. Similar differentiation tendencies emerged in the 1980s over counter-terrorism issues and more broadly the first vestiges of a European interior policy. Differentiation is glaringly obvious in the Schengen Agreement of 1985, under which a group of member states opened their mutual borders. Initially Denmark, Greece, Ireland, Italy, and the United Kingdom abstained from the initiative, which thus included only five of the then ten member states. The more important the EC became the harder it was to get all member states on board.

Greenland's decision to leave the EC, which it had joined in 1973 as part of the Kingdom of Denmark, can also be read in the context of this centrifugal counter-motion to the dominant process of deepening and enlargement. The EC's fisheries policy was a particular bone of contention and ultimately sparked the request for a looser relationship with the EC. Since 1985 Greenland has been an associated territory rather than an integral part of a member state. Like Algeria, the Greenland case reminds us that Brexit was not the first time a territorial entity decided to leave, although the difference between a large, fully fledged member state like the United Kingdom and territories brought into membership in the context of colonialism cannot be disregarded.

Next to nobody even noticed Greenland had left, as all eyes turned to Maastricht. While the original EEC treaty had remained largely unchanged for thirty years, another new treaty was now in the works just five years after the SEA. The fall of the Iron Curtain, the collapse of the Soviet Union, and German unification had radically transformed the coordinates of European and global geopolitics and enormously stepped up the pressure to reform the EC. The new geopolitical context accelerated negotiations within the Community – which in the past had often dragged on for decades – and frequently spurred their conclusion. The form and timing of the Maastricht Treaty essentially represented the outcome of that dramatic transition at the end of the Cold War, even if the agenda associated with Maastricht picked up many threads that had been around since at least the early 1980s.

In this confluence of longer-term developments and geopolitical turbulence, the Community became the central instrument for shaping western Europe's transition to the post-Cold War era. At Maastricht the European Community renamed itself the European Union. The treaty signed on 7 February 1992 went a great deal further than the programme of the SEA, creating a single structure with three pillars: the European Community, the Common Foreign and Security Policy, and Justice and Home Affairs. The European Community comprised the Single Market, the Common Agricultural Policy, Euratom, and the Economic and Monetary Union; the latter had been decades in the making and possessed the potential to catapult integration far beyond its existing bounds. The fact that agriculture was now merely one element in a pillar underlined how far its star had fallen.

Finding a solution was not easy, particularly for this first pillar. Top-level negotiations on the reform programme began at the end of 1989 and were intimately bound up with the question of German unification, which unsettled several governments – most notably British Prime Minister Margaret Thatcher. A consensus of sorts emerged in the talks between Kohl, Mitterrand, US President George Bush, and others in 1990: deeper European integration would defuse objections to German unification. Commission President Delors backed the strategy for Brussels, but its most important advocate was German Chancellor Helmut Kohl – so it was in no sense imposed on Germany. While dramatic events unfolded blow by blow and the public struggled to keep up, the emerging consensus among the heads of state and government fundamentally laid out the path to the shared currency, the euro.

Many questions remained open, especially concerning the currency policy at the heart of the treaty. The euro was to be introduced in three stages, with the third starting in 1999. Again, this was a projection into the future, not a programme for immediate implementation. At the same time the United Kingdom under Thatcher's successor John Major won an opt-out clause on the strength of British scepticism towards this decidedly supranational project. While the concession was necessary to avoid a

British veto, the clause kept the possibility of British participation open. The Danish government insisted on a similar arrangement. Yet again, the more that was at stake the less likely it was that all the partners would participate.

The second pillar was the Common Foreign and Security Policy. The CFSP built on long experience with the EPC, placing it on a new legal footing and for the first time explicitly formulating the objective of a common policy in this area. The third pillar, Justice and Home Affairs, had also been gestating for some time. Developments that had emerged formally outside the Community were now repackaged and elaborated. But the outcome fell well short of the political union that Helmut Kohl for example had wanted to establish alongside the Economic and Monetary Union. All in all, the second and third pillars were considerably less substantial than the first. They were organised in a straightforward intergovernmental fashion, whereas policies in the first pillar had strong supranational components.

The Maastricht Treaty was a compromise, reached after an epic political struggle. The Dutch proposed integrating the supranational components more organically, with a tree structure rather than pillars as the metaphor. Their suggestion was shot down in negotiations on 30 September 1991, which the disappointed Dutch dubbed 'Black Monday'.[5] As so often, the European project ultimately opted for a kind of middle line. The new European Union represented a first answer to the conundrums created by the collapse of the Eastern bloc. But

---

[5] On the 'Zwarte Maandag', see, for instance, 'EG-ministers akkoord over rol parlement', *De Telegraaf*, 13 November 1991.

3 Transformation by Stealth, 1969–1992

the treaty did not itself bring about the eastern enlargement, nor did it even prepare the EU adequately for such a step. It reflected the preceding decades of cooperation in western Europe and the sudden geopolitical shifts of 1989–1990 but did not yet build a viable framework for a Union extending across the former Iron Curtain. It did point in that direction, however, and signalised the EU's ambition to play a central role in shaping the new post-Cold War world.

Even if the Maastricht Treaty has always been visualised as a classical Greek temple with three load-bearing columns (Figure 3.8), the Union it created was more like a rickety old house with layers of successive alterations

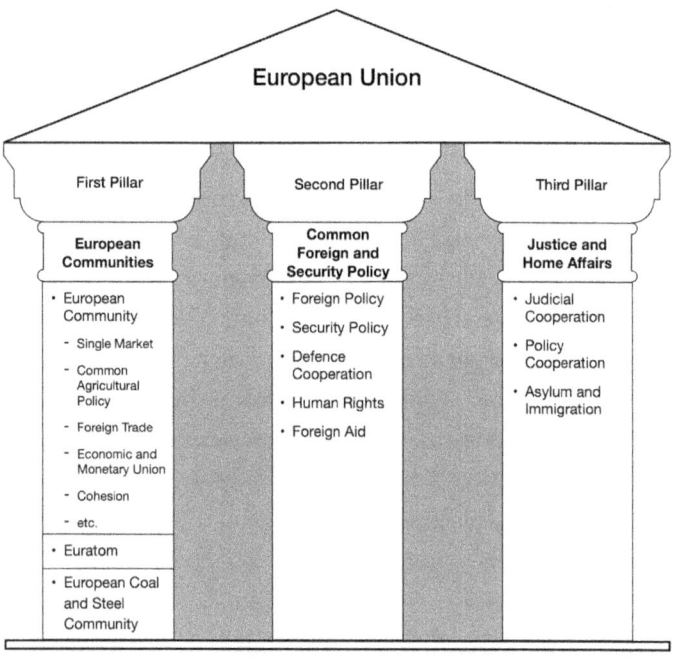

FIGURE 3.8 The 'temple' of the Maastricht Treaty (1992).

and extensions, windows and rooms added later or bricked up, and boundaries only vaguely delineated. It was the exact opposite of a precise architectural design – and that is probably what made it so significant and resilient. Instead of presenting a united front, the organisation frequently appeared as a quarrelling, garrulous gang. It brought together representatives of different states in a context where nationality was by no means automatically the determining factor. Sometimes political and ideological affinities were more important: federalists, technocrats, conservatives, social democrats, and many others were involved, as were representatives of different generations with their respective experiences and expectations. Even more than before, the EU became the stage on which intergovernmental negotiating processes and international political dramas played out. Non-state actors such as major corporations, media outlets, and trade unions also left their mark. As ever, the EU was more than just the platform for or instrument of national interests. Its diffuseness frequently permitted it to represent more than the sum of the positions of its member states and to pursue an independent course of its own. The EU created in Maastricht sometimes resembles a puppet whose strings are pulled by the most powerful, sometimes Superman, and sometimes Robert Musil's *Man Without Qualities*: an actor with great potential and a sense of possibility searching for a meaningful existence.

All this underlines how utterly unlikely it appeared, for such a long time, that the EC (later EU) would grow into Europe's most important international forum. There was no master plan for gradually building it into the leading organisation, profiting from the experience of others and a kind of division of labour at the international level, and leaving its rivals behind. All this came about through a multitude of negotiations and hard-fought struggles. Project Europe did not always come out of these fights the winner – but it did astonishingly often, especially in the dramatic phase between the mid-1980s and the Maastricht Treaty. Building on processes established over the two previous decades, it now began to shape its member states at a fundamental level, and for the first time to exert systemic influence on their fates – for better or worse.

Questions

1. Which main factors explain why the EC became the primary (and increasingly also the dominant) forum of integration in (western) Europe?
2. What was the specific significance of the 1973 EC enlargement round?
3. The early 1980s are often seen as a highly problematic period in the history of European integration. Discuss.

4

Seeking Freedom, 1992–2009

∼

The energy released by the collapse of communism and the end of the Cold War poured into the Europe integration process: a rapidly unfolding sequence of events confirmed and consolidated the trajectory of the preceding transformation phase. The euro, Schengen, multiple enlargement rounds, and the like no longer stood merely for a quantitative and geographical expansion of the EU's powers and reach. Now they breathed a new quality into European integration, in a form that was increasingly tangible to the public. From the early 1990s this led to a fundamental politicisation of the European Union, the organisation's new umbrella term since the Maastricht Treaty of 1992. Previously integration had occasionally been the subject of intense political debate, in specific phases, contexts, or regions – such as the British membership referendum in 1975, in connection with the CAP, and in the 1970s in Spain, Portugal, and Greece. Now conflicts engendered a broader politicisation that fundamentally shaped the integration process. In all these respects the early 1990s concluded a period of transformation. Moreover, the EU exhibited increasingly universalist aspirations, for instance arguing that its advocacy of free trade represented 'higher-order interests' that transcended the EU's specific positions, its own formal powers, and its institutional remit.

These high ambitions reflected a new self-confidence and sense of optimism in an era of dramatic global change. The crises of that era – some institutional, some political, and others economic – were taken very seriously at the time. But looking back from today's vantage point, they seem wonderfully inconsequential. This is the period when the EU was casting off the political and societal moorings of the Cold War era and growing into a much more meaningful entity – for better or worse.

4.1 Economics in the Driving Seat

The new Europe of the EU was as much about liberalisation as liberty. Integration continued to serve multiple goals. But, more so than during the preceding decades, a specific motif shaped the period of almost twenty years from the early 1990s to the late 2000s. The overarching theme was a specific form of far-reaching internal economic and social liberalisation, tending towards neoliberalism. The course was backed by a broad and dominant consensus in favour of supply-side economic and financial policy, further liberalisation of trade, privatisation of publicly owned enterprises, and reductions in welfare spending. All this played out during a period when globalisation became the political watchword: the promise of greater prosperity supplanted social progress as the political endgame. There were clear limits to liberalisation, however, as new forms of isolation appeared. And for a long time the social, ecological, political, and ultimately economic costs were widely ignored.

The euro, as the aspect of the EU that attracted the most attention during this period (Box 4.1), is

Box 4.1 Designing the euro

The euro was not the first common currency created by the member states of today's EU. In 1979 the European Monetary System (EMS) gave birth to the European Currency Unit, the ECU. The term sounded technocratic, as was the currency itself. The ECU was never used as cash; it was an accounting unit composed of a basket of national currencies. The euro started similarly in 1999 but entered general circulation in 2001.

Designing the notes and coins was no easy task, given the national sensitivities involved. The European Central Bank found a hybrid solution for the coins. All euro coins have a common 'European' side with the same design. Until 2006 this was a map of the EU15; in 2007, when further countries joined the euro, it was replaced with an outline of Europe. Each country chooses its own design for the 'national' side. All euro coins can be used throughout the Eurozone, irrespective of the national side. For the sake of security each denomination of euro banknote has only one design. They feature stylised images of windows, gateways, and bridges symbolising openness, cooperation, and connection. The motifs represent different periods of European history and are all invented rather than real, in order to discourage national rivalry; for the same reason no famous individuals are illustrated. All the banknotes do, however, include the signature of the serving ECB president. Altogether the notes and coins present a mix of national and European references.

emblematic of the EU's brand of liberalisation. The so-called economic and monetary union built on monetary integration policies instituted since the 1970s but raised them to a whole new level by proposing a common currency. The first of three steps took effect in July

1990 – before the Maastricht Treaty – and massively liberalised the movement of money and capital between the member states. The second stage came into effect at the beginning of 1994, initiating the establishment of the precursor of the European Central Bank (ECB) and economic reforms in the member states to fulfil the – soon to be infamous – Maastricht criteria. These defined binding convergence indicators for price inflation, state debt and budget deficits, interest rates, and exchange rate stability. The founding of the ECB itself followed in 1998. The third stage began on 1 January 1999, when eleven of the fifteen EU member states (including all six founding members) introduced the euro for accounting purposes. Exactly three years later the euro became the cash currency in twelve member states (in the meantime, Greece had also met the criteria). Now the same coins and notes circulated from Galway to Graz and Lapland to Lampedusa. The launch was an enormous economic and logistical test, which the member states passed with flying colours.

This roughly ten-year process leading to the common currency built on the optimistic dynamism of the Delors years since the mid-1980s and was expedited by the uncertainties of the end of the Cold War and German unification: anchoring Europe in a stable and substantially upgraded institutional frame gained further urgency due to these changes. At the technical level, creating the euro involved many decisions about concrete details. During the first half of the 1990s in particular its success appeared anything but certain. And in the later stages it long remained unclear which states would be permitted to join the euro club. Economic travails

4.1 Economics in the Driving Seat

made it tricky to fulfil the criteria and there were periods when the financial markets were betting on the new currency's demise. Often impasses were only resolved when the leaders took charge; the rapport between German Chancellor Helmut Kohl and the French President, first François Mitterrand and from 1995 his successor Jacques Chirac, was crucial.

Hurdles there were many. The project nearly fell apart in 1992–1993 when a European currency crisis wreaked chaos on the currency convergence required by the treaty. One important root of the problem was the German Bundesbank's policy of raising interest rates, partly on account of the costs of German unification. This caused significant stress for the other members of the European Monetary System. In September 1992, the markets began betting against the Italian lira and the British pound, which speculators like George Soros considered to be overvalued. On 16 September 1992 – 'Black Wednesday' – market pressures forced London to leave the EMS. Italy also faced serious problems but managed to stay in the system after some adjustments. Increasingly close monetary coordination and the associated implications for national economic policies came at a price, especially under the precept that annual budget deficits must never exceed 3 per cent of GDP. Budgetary rigour and spending cuts were the order of the day. The Stability and Growth Pact of 1997 only amplified this tendency. Building on a proposal by German Finance Minister Theo Waigel, the Council of the EU decided that fines could be imposed on states that violated financial discipline. Altogether the introduction of the single currency was an immense undertaking that brought the member states closer together but also generated new tensions and conflicts.

The EU's adoption of a currency policy with neoliberal components did not occur in isolation. The shift interacted with a readjustment of the macro-economic framework in the member states, which demanded great sacrifices of countries like Italy. In this process, deregulation, privatisation, and welfare cuts became bound up with the objective of the European currency. 'Europe' was repeatedly instrumentalised to shake up what were portrayed as outdated social and economic structures. The euro sharpened the pressure of competition and was supposed to make European companies more competitive in the global context. The common currency already had enormous repercussions in the preparatory phase, as the participating nation states ceded important aspects of their sovereignty to the supranational level and accepted a reduction in their influence over their national economies. The consequences for the affected societies were enormous. More than ever before the fate of national economies – especially in the Eurozone – became inseparable from that of the Union as a whole.

The euro increasingly came to represent the EU's second heart chamber alongside the Single Market. The two projects were closely connected, because a stable currency greatly facilitated trade and planning. But fundamental choices also had to be made. Unlike the Single Market, the institutional role of the Commission in the euro remained secondary. And much more importantly, many member states had been pursuing active exchange rate policies to regulate their international competitiveness.

4.1 Economics in the Driving Seat

While this school of thought characterised French currency policy for example, Germany had drawn a different lesson from history. The historical touchstones were the hyperinflation of 1923 and the currency reform of 1948 rather than the deflation of the 1930s. West Germany's economic success was attributed to the great independence of the Bundesbank and low inflation. Only if those conditions also applied to the euro was the German government willing to relinquish the deutschmark. The decision was cast in concrete in the choice of Frankfurt am Main as the seat of the European Central Bank: in Germany, close to the financial markets (and the seat of the Bundesbank), and far from the political intrigues of Brussels and the national capitals. All this gave the euro – as the EU's second heart chamber – a very German start.

In important respects the creation of a common currency was always driven more by political will than economic expertise. The convergence criteria laid out in the Maastricht Treaty prioritised achievability over economic solidity, hard as it may have been for the member states to meet the requirements. This applied especially to Greece, whose participation in the euro was initially postponed as it failed to meet the criteria; Athens only received the green light to join on 1 January 2001 – just in time for the symbolic introduction of cash a year later. But, as was later revealed, this occurred on the basis of falsified data on the Greek budget deficit. The Italian government demonstrated great determination to pursue reforms but also massaged its figures. This was an open secret in the other capitals. Belgium was little better, and even Germany was not innocent of manipulation to meet its targets. The political will to deepen the integration process and at least get all the founding members on board overrode any economic doubts. On the other side, governments revelled in the prestige of joining this exclusive club – frequently without heed to the associated costs.

Another problem arose in the medium term. Germany, as the arch enforcer, itself regularly contravened the budget criteria between 2002 and 2005, as did France. And, moreover, the two Eurozone heavyweights ensured that the sanctions for such violations were greatly watered down. The supposed culture of stability was undermined from the outset and subordinated to the liberalisation mantra, with negative medium-term consequences for all involved.

That said, the first decade of the euro certainly appeared to be beneficial for many member states. Before the common currency was introduced, the dominance of the deutschmark had left the other currencies basically dependent on the German Bundesbank; now they had a greater say in decisions. The euro facilitated trade and enabled its participants, including those who had previously placed less of a premium on stability, to borrow comparatively cheaply in the international financial markets. For a number of years this spurred growth in countries like Spain and Ireland, to an extent also in Italy and Greece; we will examine the longer-term consequences of this in the next chapter. The euro initially fell against the US dollar, but bounced back significantly from 2003, underlining its international role (Figure 4.1).

Even more importantly, the ECB was able to fulfil its primary responsibility of ensuring the euro's internal stability: inflation remained low and trade within the EU increased by more than 150 per cent between 1995 and

4.1 Economics in the Driving Seat

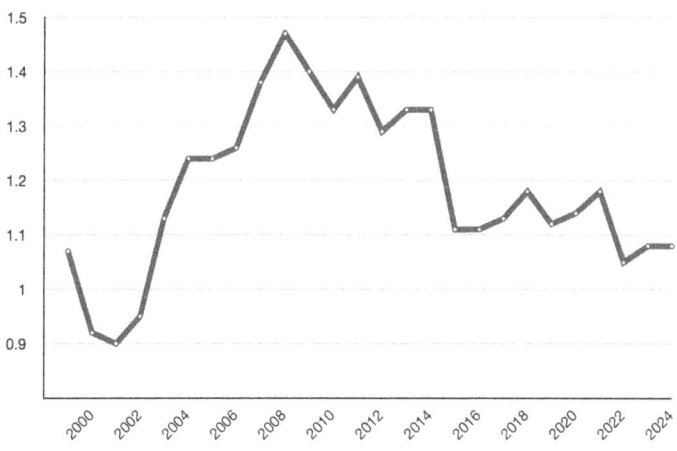

FIGURE 4.1 Euro/dollar exchange rate since 1999.

2008. While this was naturally not attributable exclusively to the euro, the single currency did make an important contribution. All in all, it fulfilled many of the hopes placed in it, while the model upon which it was based was entirely in tune with the economic ideas of the time. The common currency appeared the ideal tool for achieving growth and equalising differences between the member states. It reduced paperwork, costs, and uncertainties for businesses. Opening up new markets created opportunities but also intensified competition. Obviously, not everybody profited to the same extent. At the same time the euro created a degree of coherence and protection from global market forces by cushioning the member states from fluctuations in the dollar. Altogether the EU had become a little more independent of US hegemony in the economic sphere. For that gain, the political and economic elites in Brussels, Frankfurt, and the national capitals were quite content to accept the problems and pressures associated with the common currency.

While the euro weathered storms to emerge into the world as laid out in the Maastricht Treaty, the same cannot be said of the broader economic and political union that was also discussed at the time. Experts pointed out that the lack of closer integration in the rest of the economy left the common currency built on sand. The economies of the participating states were too disparate, they said, leading to conflicts of goals and undesirable side-effects. But their warnings went unheeded, drowned out by the euro's apparent success. The Economic and Monetary Union was missing a leg. This was all a very pale shadow of the deep political union Helmut Kohl and others envisaged complementing economic integration.

The dismantling of border controls represented an equally symbolic and consequential move. The Schengen Agreement was signed in 1985, primarily to promote the internal market. Free movement of goods was to be paired with free movement of people. Despite this ambitious agenda, border posts were not widely removed until 1995. The main reason for the delay was technical and logistical problems, which had been underestimated. In the early post-war era activists had stormed border posts to demonstrate for a united Europe. Now the open borders became a symbol of the Europe of the EU, even if – as with the euro – certain member states abstained. And like the euro, Schengen stood for the conviction, dominant at the time, that open markets would boost growth and increase prosperity for all, as well as enhancing cohesion and social stability. Concerns about immigration and crime were raised but did not dominate the debate at this point. People very quickly became used to international travel without passport controls, as if the checks

4.1 Economics in the Driving Seat

had never existed. So, Schengen and the euro were both cause and effect, they were responses to globalisation and interventions that pushed its bounds.

Schengen was a hit, with a long list of countries lining up to join its five founders. It is easy to forget that the project – like European integration altogether – proceeded in fits and starts. While Schengen has never included all the EU member states, Iceland, Norway, and Switzerland joined as non-members. When Malta, the Czech Republic, Poland, and six other central and eastern European EU states joined Schengen at the end of 2007, Polish Prime Minister Donald Tusk spoke of a 'triumph of freedom'.[1] The Cold War divide appeared to have been overcome for good, and open borders became the mantra of an ever more united Europe.

But there were definite limits to the new freedoms. The Schengen states now policed their shared external borders more strictly and their police and judicial authorities worked closely together, with the dedicated Schengen Information System playing a central role. So, the 'abolition of borders' was never unconditional or boundless, especially for states outside the Schengen group and the EU. Poles discovered what that meant in 1995, when Schengen made their borders with the EU less passable – until Poland itself joined the club only twelve years later. Frontex has been helping the member states to control their external borders since 2004, not least to repel informal migration.

This development went hand in hand with efforts to establish a common asylum system. Just as the name of

---

[1] 'Tusk: Dzisiejszy dzień jest triumfem wolności', *Gazeta Wyborcza*, 21 December 2007.

4 Seeking Freedom, 1992–2009

the Luxembourg village of Schengen is associated with freedom of movement, the Irish capital Dublin has since 1990 lent its name to the EU's rules for processing asylum applications, even more so through the follow-on regulations of 2003 and 2013. Under the Dublin II Regulation of 2003 the country in which a person first enters the EU is responsible for their asylum process. This placed the burden largely on certain Mediterranean member states. Open borders did not apply to everyone equally.

A gain in freedom tied closely to the logic of the Single Market was intimately bound up with external closure and a deeply selective and pervasive system of control. The latter was felt not only by transnational criminals. The problems faced by undocumented migrants within the EU were exacerbated by Schengen. The Senegalese-born feminist Madjiguène Cissé, who led the French *Sans Papiers* movement in the mid-1990s and helped to network it transnationally, was by no means the only one to criticise 'Fortress Europe'. Over time the idea of 'Fortress Europe' has appeared in very different guises. Before 1945 it featured occasionally in German Nazi propaganda. In the 1980s it became associated with economic protectionism. Only in the 1990s did it acquire its connection with debates over asylum and migration – initially as a negative, but since the 2020s positively connotated by far right groups.

When it came to soldiers and guns, however, the EU was not much of a fortress. Maastricht and the ensuing period did see an expansion of the Common Foreign and Security Policy (CFSP), although it fell well short of expectations. If the Single Market and the euro had

4.1 Economics in the Driving Seat

become the EU's two heart chambers, the CFSP and Schengen were the atria. Of the two, Schengen was rather more vigorous.

Like other initiatives, the CFSP did not appear out of thin air at Maastricht. Its long backstory dated to the 1970s in the European Political Cooperation, which had already been expanded under the SEA. This sphere remained intergovernmental, with important decisions requiring unanimity. The member states still had the last word on matters military and diplomatic, where – unlike currency and borders – they were not prepared to transfer such a degree of sovereignty to the EU.

Despite this caveat, the CFSP helped to make the EU more prominent than ever before on the international stage, formulating joint positions on armed conflicts, human rights, and other issues. It was learning the lesson of 1990–1991, where the EC had played no role in the decision-making about the Gulf War and had occasionally suffered hubris – for example in 1991, when Luxembourg Foreign Minister Jacques Poos declared that 'the hour of Europe has dawned' just as Yugoslavia descended into civil war and broke apart.[2] The EU proved ineffectual in the wars in ex-Yugoslavia, failing in its efforts to bring about a lasting ceasefire and peace. In the end, NATO and in particular the United States led the decisive interventions, not the European Union. So even in the CFSP there was frequently more talk than action, not least on account of the EU's military weakness. The EU's instruments turned out

---

[2] Quoted in Nicholas Watt, 'Nobel Peace Prize Leads EU to Question its Raison d'être', *The Guardian*, 12 October 2012, www.theguardian.com/world/2012/oct/12/nobel-peace-prize-eu-question-existence.

to be totally inadequate, giving rise to further reforms. In 1999, for example, the EU created the Office of the High Representative for the CFSP to beef up its foreign policy. The post existed in this form for exactly a decade and was held by Javier Solana for almost the entire time. But the member states continued to stress that this remained an intergovernmental rather than supranational matter; the High Representative was answerable to the Council of Ministers rather than the Commission (which retained its own Commissioner for External Relations). So, in global politics the EU spoke with more than one voice and its impact remained limited. Foreign and security policy continued to be the poor relations of European integration.

There were certainly projects, also in the field of defence policy. In 1999, for example, the European Council went beyond Maastricht to create a European security and defence policy, including a plan to establish a sixty-thousand-strong rapid reaction force by 2003 for international conflict prevention and intervention. Quarrelling over security issues dogged the project from the start, most spectacularly in 2003 when the question of joining the US-led invasion of Iraq deeply divided the EU eighteen months after the terrorist attack on the World Trade Center of 11 September 2001. While France, Germany, and Belgium categorically refused to participate, the United Kingdom, Italy, the Netherlands, and Spain joined the 'Coalition of the Willing', along with most of the EU accession candidates in central and eastern Europe. The European Union was deeply divided and many states experienced large anti-war demonstrations. The invasion was of highly questionable legality, the occupation and civil war created a geopolitical

4.1 Economics in the Driving Seat

disaster. But incidents such as French President Jacques Chirac's condescending comment that central and eastern European governments had missed 'a good opportunity to keep quiet'[3] were also far from helpful – the fury triggered by his remarks deepened the rift within the continent. The upshot was a devastating defeat for efforts to create a robust European security and defence policy that overshadowed comparably successful developments such as the EU Police Mission in Bosnia and Herzegovina with its police and civilian components.

In the end the EU's 'soft power' usually turned out to be more significant than its lack of military might. If the European Union made a difference, it did so above all as a civil power working globally for rule of law, multilateralism, institution building, democracy, and human rights. 'Good governance' was in vogue and shaped the Neighbourhood Policy launched in 2003. But the EU also conducted numerous civilian missions in Africa and Asia, enabling it to assert a new role in the world. Now more than ever it was truly perceived as a global actor. In the sphere of development aid the European Commission managed about 12 per cent of all international financial aid in the early 2000s, tying it more tightly than ever to democracy and human rights. EU policies vis-à-vis the wider world were increasingly backed by universalist pretensions and policymakers in Brussels especially considered the EU a force for global good.

During this period the EU intensified its ties with international organisations in other parts of the world, such

---

[3] Quoted in 'Eastern Europe Dismayed at Chirac Snub', *The Guardian*, 19 February 2003.

as the Association of Southeast Asian Nations (ASEAN). It also established new relationships, for example with the South American trade bloc MERCOSUR, founded in 1991. In each case trade matters were central, and reinforced by the GATT liberalisations in the so-called Uruguay Round of trade talks (1986–1994). Here the EU liked to see itself as a model for other regional integration initiatives, promoting their development and at the same time underlining its own leading role in global trade – also in the context of the World Trade Organization that succeeded GATT in 1994. Here, again, universalist ideas loomed large: the EU, it was asserted, had drawn the right lesson from history and others could only profit by emulating its course. Many felt that the EU's form of liberalisation was the ideal course for navigating the storms of an increasingly globalising world.

The weight of its markets made the EU an increasingly important partner for others (Figure 4.2). This was the principal route by which the EU developed into a civil power, and from the 1990s increasingly the global hegemon in the regulatory sphere. The size and appeal of its markets influenced standards in settings ranging

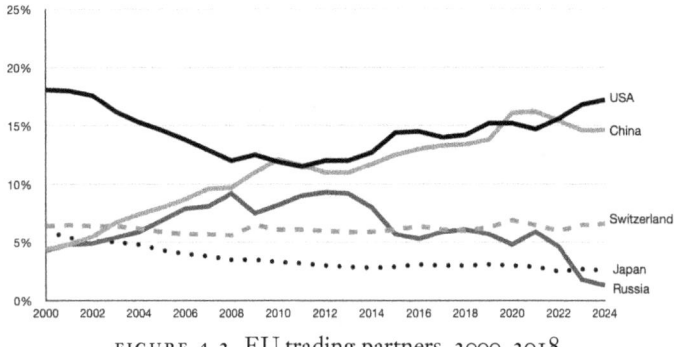

FIGURE 4.2 EU trading partners, 2000–2018.

4.1 Economics in the Driving Seat

from honey production in Brazil to the chemicals in Japanese-made toys. Despite its overt commitment to multilateralism the EU frequently acted unilaterally, demanding exacting standards in areas including environmental protection and hygiene. While this 'Brussels effect'[4] remained largely invisible, no other tool used by the EU was anywhere near as influential in its external policies.

That is not to say that the EU's model became a global paradigm or that there were no alternatives. It was also riddled with inconsistencies. The EU was much stricter on values with Myanmar than with China for example: this was the period when trade with China grew from negligible to dominant, while the relative weight of transatlantic trade declined in the 1990s and 2000s. More generally, too, the EU's orientation on values frequently clashed with its economic interests – and the latter usually won the day. For example, the trade effects of the protectionist agricultural policy violated the ideal of liberalisation. Especially in the Global South the EU looked more like an economic Leviathan than a civil power, pulling no punches to assert its interests in trade, migration, asylum, and other issues.

Whatever its impact, the EU was now playing an increasingly active civil role in global politics. One important factor here was the space that had appeared on the world stage. The United States, with which the EU and its member states remained closely allied, was now the sole superpower; Russia was in disarray after the

---

[4] Anu Bradford, *The Brussels Effect: How the European Union Rules the World* (Oxford: Oxford University Press, 2020).

collapse of the Soviet Union and the economic slump of the 1990s, while China's meteoric rise had yet to fully impact global relations. The EU had room to develop globally and to exhibit new confidence on the international stage. Terrorism aside, security concerns receded, at least in comparison to the Cold War era. And NATO still formed a robust safety net for any unlikely worst-case scenario. Economic questions ruled the day, pumping oxygen into the EU, whose rise had always hinged on the economic factor. With the cocoon of other organisations no longer needed, the EU emerged influential and optimistic, using its charm rather than resorting to force, while also remaining somehow fragile and ephemeral.

More important than its position in the world was the EU's new role vis-à-vis its own member states in contexts such as the euro, Schengen, the CFSP, and the Single Market. The latter experienced a significant realignment during this phase: while the Single Market as a whole grew steadily in importance, its agricultural appendage, which had been a key driver of European integration during long phases of the Cold War, was now pruned back a little. The MacSharry Reform of 1992, named after the Irish Commissioner for Agriculture, was a turning point for the CAP. Since its birth, it had incentivised farmers to maximise production through price guarantees. This led to expensive overproduction, which consumed up to 70 per cent of the EC's entire budget in the 1980s. The pressure for internal reforms was only heightened by the planned eastern enlargement; given the economic structures of the countries involved the costs would have been immense. Another factor was Washington's liberalisation agenda in the GATT trade talks. The MacSharry Reform

4.1 Economics in the Driving Seat

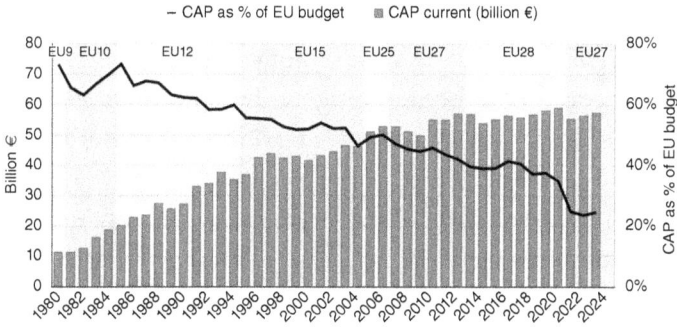

FIGURE 4.3 CAP share of EU budget since 1980.

actually increased direct payments to farmers, thus preserving the CAP's original social policy dimension. But now, environmental goals were taken into account more systematically. While the EU's agricultural policy remained highly interventionist, its agricultural market became more accessible to third-country producers from the 1990s. Even more importantly, the EU successively abolished its export subsidies, which had caused great difficulties for third-country producers. Although this did not really amount to full-spectrum liberalisation, it did represent a degree of opening and a partial adaptation of the CAP to global markets. The CAP continued to consume billions but no longer played the singular role it had through the 1970s (Figure 4.3). The former flagship of European integration was not sheltered from the new winds a-blowing.

The EU's liberalisation of the 1990s and 2000s prioritised economic means of deepening and widening European integration. Back in 1952, when the ECSC was set up, calling it a 'European' community had been rather pretentious given that it involved just six western European countries and two sectors of the economy. By the end of the century, it made much more sense to use the terms EU and Europe synonymously – and more and more people began doing so. For sure, the EU has never included all of Europe's territory and has little or no say on many issues that are central to everyday life. Still, the speed with which its role and relevance grew was stunning.

4.2 Interaction and Fragmentation

The EU's relationship to its immediate neighbourhood in the 1990s and 2000s was as crucial as its internal transformations, and more important than its links to the wider world. A series of enlargements expanded its membership from twelve to twenty-seven.

The first move, though, was not eastwards but to integrate the countries that had remained neutral throughout the Cold War. Of these, only Ireland had joined before 1989. Austria, Sweden, and Finland took the plunge in 1995, now adopting a clear stance on the new, post–Cold War Europe after a long courtship. The accession round might have been even larger, had Norway and Switzerland not pulled out after negative referendums. Instead, Norway became part of the European Economic Area, an international agreement signed in 1992 that extended the EU's Single Market to most of the remaining European Free Trade Association (EFTA) states; Switzerland was the one EFTA country that rejected this close link, instead negotiating a long series of bilateral treaties through which it adopted most but not all of the EU's legal instruments. The European Union's gravitational pull was massive. And, as before,

4.2 Interaction and Fragmentation

all the other major western European international organisations continued to exist, even if some, such as EFTA, lost most of their clout. On the other hand, the former Eastern bloc's major forums, most importantly the Warsaw Pact as the Soviet-dominated security organisation and the Council for Mutual Assistance, the bloc's economic organisation, collapsed with the end of the Cold War. This constellation made it much easier for the neutrals to join the EU.

The EU had its eye in particular on the new members' markets in the 1995 enlargement; these were prosperous societies with high per capita GDP and purchasing power. There were political motives too, of course, but EU-style liberalisation and its economic foundations played an especially important role in this fourth round of enlargement (after 1973, 1981, and 1986). Austria for example experienced a productivity boost from EU membership and strongly internationalised its economy. The EU's liberalisation policy also broke numerous state monopolies, for example in the energy and telecommunications sectors, which many, particularly among the member states' elites, saw as the right response to the challenges of globalisation.

After the neutral states, integrating the former Warsaw Pact states was high on the EU's post-Cold War agenda (noting that the territory of the former GDR had already joined the EC in 1990 in the course of German unification). Here the challenges were greater than in any previous enlargement round: economies in crisis, unfinished political transformations, and very different historical experiences. Some saw this as an argument for rapid full membership for the post-communist states, while others counselled a slower pace or shallower integration. At the end of 1989, for instance, French President François Mitterrand proposed a confederation, with a deeply integrated core EU at the heart of a more loosely connected broader entity. The idea initially attracted influential supporters. Czechoslovak President Václav Havel backed the idea in March 1990, while German Chancellor Helmut Kohl had said something similar a month earlier. The abrupt end to the Cold War obviously caught all involved unprepared.

The mood shifted rapidly, however. By March 1991 Havel was no longer willing to settle for second-class status for his country. Fears concerning Russia's future stance led many central and eastern European states to insist on full membership. The times appeared too risky for experiments. Among the existing member states, the British and increasingly also the German government agreed that rapid integration was the best means to stabilise the region and the continent as a whole and prevent the emergence of a geopolitical vacuum. Security was an important consideration for Germany, and for Chancellor Kohl personally the eastern enlargement was the logical and triumphant conclusion of the process he was so closely identified with. The British and Danish governments were more interested in expanding the Single Market and watering down other member states' supranational tendencies through enlargement. As always, national interests shaped the various positions. Ultimately, however, full integration became the dominant model – even if it was going to take time to implement.

This approach meant projecting western Europe's existing multilateral approach onto the nations of central and eastern Europe, whose governments saw things similarly. The Western political and economic model was regarded as the victor of the Cold War. Central and eastern Europe was not looking to become a laboratory of new and untried forms of international cooperation. Possible alternatives to the EU – such as confederation, a permanent central European free trade agreement, or the CSCE as the existing platform for bringing together the formerly divided parts of Europe – soon either became marginal or turned into accession vehicles. If the European Union had not acquired such outstanding importance since the 1970s it would never have become the central player in Europe's post-communist transformation.

It was not all about the EU, however. Most of the central and eastern European states joined the Council of Europe between 1990 and 1993, with Hungary leading the way in 1990. Poland and Hungary joined the OECD in 1996, and, together with the Czech Republic, became NATO members in 1999 – well before the EU's eastern enlargement of 2004. The EU was certainly not reordering Europe entirely on its own, although together with NATO it did form the decisive forum. As Lithuania's ambassador to France, Giedrius Čekuolis, put it in 2005, 'NATO and the EU are like mom and dad, and we can't choose between the two'.[5] NATO stood for integration in the West's transatlantic security system. In particular in central and eastern Europe, the EU was widely regarded as the complementary project: primarily

---

[5] Quoted in Michel Fortmann and Stéfanie von Hlatky, 'NATO Enlargement 20 Years On: Some Thoughts', *Policy Brief* 10, Network for Strategic Analysis, April 2021, https://ras-nsa.ca/nato-enlargement-20-years-on-some-thoughts/ (accessed 1 May 2025).

economic in focus, but also borne by shared history, perspectives, and values.

The principal reason that the EU took so much longer than other international organisations to admit the former Eastern bloc states lay in its uniquely deep integration. The accessions were only consummated after a long courtship guided by association agreements, of which the first with post-communist states were concluded at the end of 1991. The Union first had to make sure it was ready for this enlargement, and of course the post-communist states had even more work to do. Enlargement thus represented a central motivation for the many post-Maastricht treaty reforms (to which we will return); the accession candidates were required to fulfil the Copenhagen criteria of June 1993, with transformative effects. And Brussels kept a close watch on their progress towards meeting a raft of standards concerning their economic order, rule of law, and human rights. Within fifteen years of the fall of the Berlin Wall this route brought most of the post-communist countries of central and eastern Europe into the EU, along with Cyprus and Malta.

The official accession talks with the Czech Republic, Cyprus, Estonia, Hungary, Poland, and Slovenia began in 1998, followed by Bulgaria, Latvia, Lithuania, Malta, Romania, and Slovakia in early 2002. By 1999 the Commission agreed that all the applicants had met the relevant political criteria; in 2002 it confirmed the same for the economic and legislative criteria for ten of them – which many western European leaders would have ruled out just a few years earlier. In the end, Cyprus, the Czech Republic, Estonia, Hungary, Latvia, Lithuania, Malta,

4.2 Interaction and Fragmentation

Poland, Slovakia, and Slovenia joined on 1 May 2004, with Bulgaria and Romania following on 1 January 2007.

This process enjoyed broad public support in the accession countries. Some of the approval referendums were won by enormous margins: in Lithuania and Slovakia over 90 per cent, in Slovenia only slightly less. The celebrations in 2004 were correspondingly euphoric. Latvian Foreign Minister Sandra Kalniete spoke of 'Europe's triumph over the twentieth century'.[6] This was a time of rediscovering the continent's shared history, of a narrative of learning from the fatal mistakes of the past, and of boundless optimism about Europe's future. Joining the EU was frequently referred to as 'returning to Europe', as historical narratives fused with desire for change. What had originally started out as a small technical international organisation was now increasingly identified with the entire continent.

But not everyone was euphoric. The conflict over support for the Iraq War and the deep rifts it had created in Europe were still raw. The 2004 European Parliament elections, the first after the eastern enlargement, saw turnout hit a historic low of 46.5 per cent; in the Czech Republic, Estonia, and Poland it was under 30 per cent, in Slovenia a mere 17 per cent. Enormous transformation problems affecting ordinary people crushed the great hopes that many governments had placed in accession. In Poland for example the Kaczyński brothers' Eurosceptic-leaning PiS (Prawo i Sprawiedliwość, 'Law and Justice Party' in English) won the 2005 presidential election. At

---

[6] Quoted in Wilfried Loth, *Building Europe: A History of European Unification* (Berlin: De Gruyter, 2015), p. 376.

the same time the West was revelling in its own success. But there were also fears over cheap labour and transfer payments to the new member states, as well as worries that the existing institutional structures would be unable to cope with the enlargement. Nowhere, interestingly, were the reservations as strong as in the unified Germany, where the impending eastern enlargement of May 2004 was supported by only 28 per cent. Here there was no difference between the former West Germany and the eastern part of the country that had itself only become part of the EU fourteen years earlier.

The eastern enlargement of 2004 made the EU the world's most important single market. Its population grew by one fifth to 450 million and the Iron Curtain was gone for good. By the first half of the 2000s the most prosperous post-communist states were already catching up with the poorest members elsewhere in terms of per capita GDP – compare Portugal and Greece with Estonia and Slovenia in 2005. These rates of growth were not exclusively attributable to the accession perspective of course, but it was an important factor, as seen in the spike in foreign direct investment immediately following the decision to pursue eastern enlargement. Successes in fighting corruption and creating viable administrative structures also played a role. These effects were most obvious in comparison to eastern European states without any concrete accession perspective, such as Belarus. So, the eastern enlargement was a success in many respects.

But it was also a brutal transition. The EU's mantra was liberalise, deregulate, privatise, with predictable consequences for structures and services. The EU was

4.2 Interaction and Fragmentation

not pushing that line alone of course: the economic programme was propagated globally by the International Monetary Fund and the World Bank under the so-called Washington consensus – a set of economic prescriptions revolving around free-market policies. And even more importantly, these policies were not simply imposed by outsiders. Parts of the elites of these societies were also true believers, such as Poland's first post-communist Finance Minister Leszek Balcerowicz and his Czechoslovak counterpart Václav Klaus, who went on to become the Czech Republic's first prime minister just a few years later. The Balcerowicz Plan of October 1989 set out to convert Poland's centrally planned system into a free-market economy. The Warsaw government told its citizens there was simply no alternative to shock therapy.

The transformations had grave repercussions. Jobs were lost, ways of life destroyed, many emigrated to find work. Liberalisation generated enormous insecurity, benefited the strong, and exacerbated inequalities. The transformation process produced clear winners and losers. In the medium term this would come back to haunt its instigators, undermining social stability, democratic legitimacy, and the European integration process.

The EU both drew on and advanced neoliberalism. In Poland the Balcerowicz Plan abolished protections for state-owned firms, limited wage increases in the state-owned sector, and abolished the state monopoly in international trade. This helped to pave the way for the EU's Single Market with its credo of liberalisation. The EU was not just neoliberal, though. Its institutions did at least ameliorate the side-effects to the extent that they insisted on

4 Seeking Freedom, 1992–2009

FIGURE 4.4 Various EU member states profited from the Cohesion Funds. Here is an example from the Azores.
Credit: European Commission.

strong democratic institutions, rule of law, and at least minimal social benefits. And significant funding flowed eastwards. During the preparatory phase the post-communist states were already receiving extensive economic aid. Between 1990 and 2006 the countries that were to join in 2004 and 2007 received a total of €18.7 billion. Small potatoes against the Federal Republic's spending on the former GDR perhaps, but still a significant amount of money at the time. The Regional Development Fund, along with the new Cohesion Fund established in 1994, played a significant role in reducing development disparities after accession (Figure 4.4). The same applied to the agricultural budget. The EU's liberalisation was implemented not as a rigid neoliberal project but cushioned and corrected. Without the EU the social consequences of the transformation would have been a great deal worse.

4.2 Interaction and Fragmentation

These processes changed the West too. The liberalisation agenda in central and eastern Europe also created pressures affecting the 'old' member states. This applied especially to countries like Germany, Austria, and Sweden, which had particularly close exchange and intense competition with central and eastern Europe. Germany was a special case, where unification meant that the Western and post-communist worlds met within the country. From the early 2000s the cost of transfer payments and liberalisation effects was increasingly felt in the former West Germany too. But Germany is only the most obvious example of a broader phenomenon; the transformation of the post-communist societies brought about a 'co-transformation'[7] in Europe, east and west, in which the EU played an important enabling function.

The liberalisation was not boundless, however, and a string of transitional arrangements were instituted. One of these was to exempt the new member states temporarily from some of the EU's strict environmental standards (which they would have been unable to fulfil). This represented another means to cushion some of the legal consequences of membership, in this case by postponement rather than transfer payments and infrastructure assistance.

The 'old' member states certainly ensured their interests were served. Most of them, including Germany and France, insisted on a delay of up to seven years before allowing free movement of labour from the new member states. Fearing

---

[7] Philipp Ther, *Europe since 1989: A History* (Princeton: Princeton University Press, 2018).

that otherwise their own labour markets would be destabilised by workers from the new member states, they resisted and slowed the co-transformation to which the central and eastern European societies were so defencelessly exposed. Only Ireland, Sweden, and the United Kingdom chose to do without such protections. The British case is especially interesting. Despite his reputation as an opponent of (over)ambitious European integration, Prime Minister Tony Blair permitted immediate and unrestricted labour immigration from within the EU for a mix of moral and economic reasons. The number of EU migrants in the United Kingdom rose from 1.5 million in 2004 to 3.5 million in 2016, when the Brexit referendum saw immigration become a central issue for the leave campaign.

So, European integration also contained the potential to drive member states apart. And even if the enlargement dynamic did not lead to a radical restructuring, it certainly generated enormous pressure and tectonic shifts.

In light of these fundamental changes, it is no surprise that the process of European integration met with greater public interest – and stiffer resistance – from the 1990s. The first signs of trouble appeared in the ratification process for the Maastricht Treaty in 1992–1993. The Danish referendum in June 1992 produced a tiny margin of 50.7 per cent against the treaty; the yes vote in France was slim and parliamentary ratification in the United Kingdom was close-run. The Danes 'changed their minds' in a second referendum after the country was granted opt-outs. But the damage had been done. To this day Maastricht is seen as a portent that brought many other conflicts in its train.

4.2 Interaction and Fragmentation

The strong and growing expectations are reflected most clearly in the fundamental treaties of European integration (Box 4.2). Maastricht and its successors – the Treaties of

Box 4.2 The failed Constitutional Treaty

After the Nice Treaty of 2001 left most parties unsatisfied, the European Council decided to launch a new debate about the (institutional) future of Europe. Instead of an intergovernmental conference, a convention was charged with drafting a Constitutional Treaty. The convention was chaired by former French President Valéry Giscard d'Estaing and composed of European and national parliamentarians from member and applicant states as well as representatives of national governments and the Commission. It deliberated in public and produced the draft of a Constitutional Treaty for a substantially deepened European Union. Complicated intergovernmental negotiations led to amendments, for instance on voting procedures and the distribution of powers. To the disappointment of some, there was no explicit reference to Christianity in the preamble of the draft treaty's final version. Representatives of the member states signed the treaty in an official ceremony in Rome in October 2004. Despite its name, the new treaty would not have transformed the EU into a state. The member states ultimately remained in charge and, as always, the text represented a compromise relying on incremental change.

Before the treaty could enter into force all member states had to ratify it according to their specific constitutional arrangements and political processes. In most member states that meant a vote in parliament, but several chose or were required to hold referendums. The result of the French referendum on 29 May 2005 – held after various member states had already ratified – sent shock waves through Europe. The French rejected the draft treaty by 55 per cent to 45 per cent.

Three days later the Dutch referendum result was 62 per cent against and just 38 per cent in favour of the treaty. Two of the six founding member states of the EU had come out against the new treaty. Its opponents were not necessarily against the EU – the choice was between the status quo or the new arrangement, not leaving the Union. Lack of knowledge and domestic factors unrelated to the draft's actual substance help to explain the outcome, although some did genuinely oppose the deeper form of integration the draft treaty stood for.

The French 'non' and the Dutch 'nee' killed the Constitutional Treaty, at least in its original form. After a two-year 'reflection period', European leaders tried again, this time producing the Lisbon Treaty of 2007. It adopted many elements of its failed predecessor, including doing away with the pillar structure of the Maastricht Treaty. Instead, the Lisbon Treaty forged a single, consolidated legal personality. But it refrained from suggesting that it was the EU's constitution.

Amsterdam (1997) and Nice (2001), the (ultimately abandoned) Constitutional Treaty (2004), and the Treaty of Lisbon (signed 2007, effective from 2009) – each involved a further deepening of the integration process and certain adaptations to the post-Cold War world. They also succeeded in bringing into the treaty framework many developments that had emerged outside them. This process first appeared with the Single European Act of 1987; now for example the Treaty of Amsterdam integrated the Schengen Agreement into the EU's legal framework.

Although the process fell short of radical restructuring, there was a broad consensus that a reform treaty was the ideal means for advancing the cause. The SEA of 1987 had been the first foray in that direction, in retrospect marking the launch of two decades of reform efforts culminating in the Treaty of Lisbon. That was a step change after thirty years operating on the basis of the original treaties with adjustments consistently kept below the threshold of fundamental reform. The road from the SEA to Lisbon was in the end a series of 'almosts': never the full monty but always inching towards closer union. Until Lisbon the pro-integration camp consistently freighted each next step with ever greater expectations, making disappointments inevitable. The same applied to the outcomes. The worst defeats were those where the negotiated text failed to complete the ratification process, as in the case of the Constitutional Treaty, rejected in French and Dutch referendums in 2005. All in all, the initiatives to place the EU on a new institutional footing were fragile and half-baked.

The reform debates were not only about powers for the EU as a whole but also the relative influence of the member states, for example the allocation of European Parliament seats or Commission posts. Haggling over national interests often obscured the fundamental problem of how to make the EU more democratic, more transparent, more accessible, and more efficient, and how to adapt it for the post-Cold War world. These discussions were more politicised and often more toxic than in previous decades, which many observers interpreted as a sign of crisis. But debates are a natural part of politics. For all the problems and controversies, the new levels of attention and controversy also reflected the magnitude of the stakes in an ever larger and ever more diverse Union.

Another driver of the reform process was growing public criticism of the achievements to date. One major concern was to address the EU's democratic deficits and engender public ownership of the shared European project. For example, Maastricht created a European Union citizenship (alongside the national) symbolised by a uniform passport format. The European Parliament was granted expanded powers. 'Citizens' initiatives' were established as an instrument of participatory democracy at the European level. More visible than such mechanisms was the EU's growing symbolic presentation – with flag and anthem – and the labelling of a treaty as a 'constitution' – which it was patently not. But none of these (failed) attempts to popularise the EU politically and symbolically could get at the roots of the problems.

Social policy initiatives sought to close the gap between the institutions and the citizens but made no meaningful headway. During the Cold War any moves to balance the free-market slant of European integration by introducing more redistributive elements were restricted to individual sectors such as the Common Agricultural Policy or specific geographical areas, for instance under the banner of the EU's regional policy. Ambitious proposals by the Delors Commission in the second half of the 1980s came to naught, with the exception of the Social Chapter in the Maastricht process, which set out minimum employment standards. Integration in the social sphere remained extremely controversial and British objections kept the Social Chapter out of the Maastricht Treaty itself. Although things changed a little with the Treaty of Amsterdam a few years later, the EU's social policy powers were tightly constrained compared to Schengen, the Single Market, or the euro. The heavy lifting continued to be done by programmes at the national level and most member states showed little inclination

4.2 Interaction and Fragmentation

to transfer powers in this field to the Union. The most obvious opening for Brussels to intervene was when it could present social initiatives as imperative to protect economic competitiveness and growth. The EU's greatest social policy leverage lay elsewhere, in jurisprudence rather than redistribution, as evidenced by measures in areas as disparate as health and safety at work, consumer rights, and anti-discrimination. Rhetorically, and frequently also in practice, social policy was still subsidiary to liberalisation and markets.

Gender equality is a good example. The 1957 Treaties of Rome included a call for equal pay for equal work. But its impact was limited, and the EU's influence on gender equality should not be overstated. Other factors were salient, too, and several member states had anchored the principle in national law before 1957. Apparently, the EU lacks the requisite instruments and the objective remains unfulfilled to this day.

Paradoxically, though, the debate about a 'European social model' continued through the 1990s and 2000s. But what it actually involved remained vague and contested. Nevertheless, the EU was seen as a potentially important actor in this field and much more was expected of it than during the Cold War. The debate assumed a strongly political character, although consensus over agenda and orientation remained out of reach. As in other areas, integration already went too far for some, not nearly far enough for others; some felt the EU was too neoliberal, others too protectionist; fundamental criticism came from both right and left. It was the classical dilemma, with no clear majority for the status quo but none for plausible corrections either.

In other fields, the EU's powers grew more smoothly. In environmental policy for instance the Union acquired far-reaching competences and instituted a growing number of legal acts. Here the major treaties were less important than the so-called secondary legislation, the continuous output of regulations, directives, and other legal acts. It was these that made the EU a force to be reckoned with on environmental matters, rising above purely national environmental legislation. Globally, the EU overtook the United States as a regulatory leader in this field (although in fairness it should also be noted that the implementation of EU law often remained patchy). Even more significantly, none of the measures were enough to achieve the goal of sustainable development laid out in the Treaties of Maastricht and Amsterdam.

In view of these differences, the debates over decision-making procedures and the roles of the various EU organs were heated. Sometimes because of institutional shifts, sometimes because of the many challenges in shaping a post-Cold War world, the European Council became more central from the 1990s, and above all more visible in the media than ever before. That also ramped up the potential for public disappointment when leaders failed to achieve agreement. At the same time the Commission and Parliament were granted additional powers and expanded their roles, which intensified and fine-tuned the interplay of the different parts, but also tended to make progress more difficult. For example, the Treaty of Amsterdam increased the sway of the Commission president vis-à-vis the other commissioners, giving him or her a say in their selection and responsibility for the allocation of portfolios. This strengthened the

4.2 Interaction and Fragmentation

Commission president's position vis-à-vis the Council; but the Council's choice of Commission president must be confirmed by the Parliament. The latter also campaigned successfully to expand its powers. This was seen especially in 1999 when the European Parliament forced the resignation of Jacques Santer's entire Commission over a corruption scandal. That was unprecedented. This incident further strengthened the Parliament – but did little to enhance the reputation of the EU as a whole. In other words, there was a continuous rebalancing of power between the EU institutions, but without making them any more transparent.

The human factor also played an important role in these processes, as it did in all other spheres of European integration. For example, Jacques Delors was so successful as Commission president because he was able to win over the decisive member states in the Council, especially during his first term. His successor Jacques Santer trod much more cautiously. Santer's Italian successor Romano Prodi found it difficult, as the former prime minister of a major state, to find his way into the role, which weakened the Commission's ties to the Council. Personalities certainly shaped processes and outcomes, and finding viable compromises was always hard.

In view of the scale of the challenges, the proposed solutions were frequently presented as inevitable. The insistence that there were no alternatives contributed to continuously falling turnout at European elections and provoked frustration and criticism. One frequent objection was that when a treaty was rejected by national referendum it was simply put to the vote again without major alterations. The path from the failed Constitutional

Treaty to the Lisbon Treaty is one example. Other obvious cases come from 1992, when the Danish 'nej' in the Maastricht referendum led to opt-out causes and a second, successful referendum, and 2008, when the Irish electorate rejected the Lisbon Treaty – only to accept it sixteen months later in a second referendum, after some changes and guarantees. No wonder then if many people perceived the EU as a technocratic elite project where their opinions counted for little. As today, one fundamental reason for the failure to realise incisive reforms was that the *acquis communautaire* reconciled widely diverging interests and rested on arcane compromises. This package cannot be undone without risking the very existence of the organisation. The institutions saw their powers and responsibilities expand at the same time as they were told to become leaner and more transparent. In practice that frequently meant squaring the circle. In view of the tight constraints and successive crises it is astonishing that the EU never ground completely to a halt.

As the European Union's significance for national and international politics grew, even minor questions and projects became big issues and were politicised as never before. The Services in the Internal Market Directive of 2006 is a case in point. No previous directive had ever drawn such public criticism. Also referred to as the Bolkestein Directive after the commissioner responsible, the Dutchman Frits Bolkestein, the draft of 2004 set out to liberalise the service sector, where national law had hitherto preserved many obstacles to the logic of a common market. Bolkestein's draft provoked massive resistance in Germany, Belgium, Luxembourg, Sweden, and especially France. The criticism became embodied in

4.2 Interaction and Fragmentation

FIGURE 4.5 Polish tourism poster from 2005, playing on the 'Polish plumber' trope: 'I'm staying in Poland. Come to us!'

the figure of the 'Polish plumber', the spectre of cheap competition from central and eastern Europe eroding employment conditions and social standards (Figure 4.5). Correspondingly, the project was backed by countries with more highly liberalised service sectors like the United Kingdom and the Netherlands, as well as the new post-communist member states. The latter especially hoped that the neoliberal 'shock therapy' of the 1990s would be rewarded with expanded market access. The opponents came out on top and the directive ultimately adopted in 2006 was less radical than the original draft. That said, it still represented a further liberalisation, for example in the food industry, with notable consequences for the labour market.

The critics of Bolkestein's plan were well aware that it formed part of a broader agenda. His directive was one of the first steps for implementing the so-called Lisbon Strategy adopted by the heads of state and government in March 2000. The objective of this key statement of the EU's style of liberalisation and globalisation strategy was to transform the EU within a decade into 'the most competitive and dynamic knowledge-based economy in the world'.[8] First and foremost this meant increasing productivity and speeding up innovation. As well as its neoliberal aspects, the agenda also incorporated classical social democratic elements, for example in its ideas for fighting mass unemployment. But ultimately the free-market creed predominated. Within just a few years globalisation-critical protests against the Lisbon Strategy spurred the 2005 referendum defeats for the Constitutional Treaty in France and the Netherlands. Another five years later the EU had to admit that it had failed to implement the ten-year agenda set in 2000.

Opposition to neoliberalism grew across the board in the 2000s, especially because removing barriers to the Single Market required the institution of new rules. Liberalisation needed regulation, which is why national and European neoliberal initiatives rarely led to a dismantling of administrative structures. This quickly flared into withering criticism of the allegedly faceless, squid-like Brussels bureaucracy. The transformation that had immensely expanded the EU's role since the 1980s was now in plain sight – and many people found themselves wondering when they had actually agreed to this.

---

[8] Presidency Conclusions, Lisbon European Council, 23 and 24 March 2000, www.consilium.europa.eu/uedocs/cms_data/docs/pressdata/en/ec/00100-r1.en0.htm (accessed 1 May 2025).

4.2 Interaction and Fragmentation

Although France and Germany often set the pace and direction, they were not the driving forces behind the politicisation and fundamental questioning of European integration. Important momentum came instead from Italy, where a decades-old pro-integration consensus was crumbling, and from the new member states. Many post-communist states saw sceptics asking pointedly whether European integration was not intervening too deeply in their newly won national sovereignty. Such arguments were put forward for example by the PiS in Poland and by the Czech liberal Václav Klaus, who also excoriated the Brussels bureaucracy. In a different historical context, insistence on the national had always characterised the British and Danish positions, and now that current received fresh blood. The growth of populist right-wing parties and movements was a case in point. In Austria the formerly pro-integration Freedom Party did a U-turn in the course of the 1990s. Now they campaigned on fear of foreign criminals and loss of national identity. Ethnonationalism was on the march, especially in central and eastern Europe where there was less of a welfare safety net to cushion the transformation shock. There was no clear East–West divide, though. In the Baltic states, for example, criticism of integration was never particularly strong. Moreover, many of the ideas and actors behind the push for national sovereignty hailed from the western member states.

This growing dissonance also encouraged moves towards differentiated integration, whose rudiments date back to the 1970s. In central areas – Schengen, the euro, and social policy – certain EU member states abstained from participation. This tendency to fragmentation increased in the

4 Seeking Freedom, 1992–2009

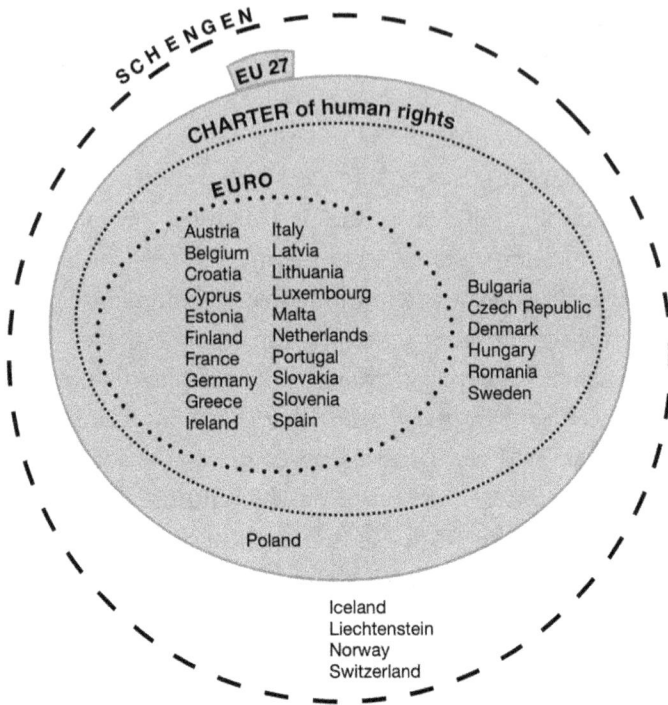

FIGURE 4.6 Differentiated Europe: an incomplete summary (2000). Further layers of differentiation have been added over the past two decades.

1990s to a point where around half of all EU policies were differentiated in some form or other (Figure 4.6). That only made the problems of democratic legitimacy and transparency all the more pressing. Initially differentiation was regarded as a transient phenomenon: a group of pioneers would lead the way and the rest would soon follow. But by the 2000s there was growing realisation that the problem was not going away. And that only exacerbated the problem of transparency and democratic deficits.

A countervailing trend to this form of liberalisation existed in debates revolving closely around the issue of

4.2 Interaction and Fragmentation

European identity. These possessed a normative core, for instance in discussions about whether potential accession candidates fulfilled the Copenhagen criteria. Sometimes this mingled with essentialist arguments, for example where a country was assumed to be fundamentally different. That applied in particular to Turkey. Back in 1963, the EC concluded an association agreement with Turkey that held out the prospect of full membership. An application submitted in 1987 was rejected in 1989, but in 1999 Turkey was granted the status of accession candidate. Official accession talks were opened in 2005 but accompanied by a raging debate about whether Turkey with its Muslim majority was compatible with the EU, whether it was 'European' enough. That had interested exactly nobody in 1963. There was also the issue of whether the EU would be overstretching itself. Although the negotiations formally continued, Turkey and the EU drifted increasingly apart. Fractures appeared over the question of enlargement, and in relation to the underlying values and economic benefits of European integration.

All in all, the EU's approach to liberalisation remained within clear bounds in the fifteen years after the Maastricht Treaty. Nevertheless, the spectrum of debates and practices it coloured is striking. This was a tendency that arose through the interaction of very different interests, challenges, and strategies. Frequently it was not a proactive force but became relevant in responses to crisis and fundamental change – such as turbulence in the international monetary system, the end of the Cold War, or the pressures of globalisation. Its essence lay in the sphere of the economy, and it tended to regard economic levers as obvious means to overcome crises, for example through freer markets, a common currency, or trade liberalisation. Thus, the EU mutated into a pacemaker and transmission belt of globalisation. This was felt especially in the Global South, where the 2003 Cotonou Agreement replaced the Lomé Conventions and reaffirmed power asymmetries. The EU created social policies for the citizens of its own member states, but these were never able to make meaningful headway against the logic of the markets. Moreover, they mostly applied to citizens while the situation was very different for (undocumented) migrants. Also, its environmental policies always remained secondary to economic goals.

In retrospect many Europeans tend to see this as a quiet and successful phase of the European project, where the institutions made great progress and benefited from the favourable conditions of the time. Having said this, the European project was not without its problems. Many reforms remained incomplete, where member states found themselves unable to agree a truly viable European solution yet unwilling to opt unequivocally for national sovereignty. Examples include the flimsy structures behind the euro and the inadequacies of the migration and asylum policy. The integration process advanced, but it had not been storm proofed.

For many citizens the first two post-Cold War decades were characterised by fundamental and challenging transformations, especially in the former Eastern bloc. The institutional crises – such as the resignation of the Santer Commission in 1999 and the failure of the Constitutional Treaty in 2005 – seem trivial compared to what was to come from the late 2000s. And yet even back then there was often talk of crisis or even a possible disintegration of the Union. Despite wars in ex-Yugoslavia and other parts of the world and terrorist attacks, including Madrid 2004 and London 2005, security issues were still on the back burner. That was about to change. In the coming period securing the EU's achievements – and security itself – would top the agenda.

Questions

1. Why did the EU become more politicised than ever before from the early 1990s? Is this development problematic or positive?
2. Summarise and explain the reasons why some wanted the 2004 EU enlargement round and others opposed it.
3. What does differentiated integration mean? Discuss its pros and cons.

5
Security First

Course Correction, since 2009

~

The integration process has always been shaped – and often spurred – by crises. No decade passed without turmoil. At the institutional level this included the Empty Chair Crisis in the 1960s and the constitutional referendum defeats of 2005, while global economic downturn affected European integration in the 1970s. International conflicts also shaped developments, as during the wars in ex-Yugoslavia in the 1990s. All three forms of crisis have also been in play since the late 2000s, their magnitude, frequency, and pace having accelerated enormously. Sometimes European politics feels like one long disaster movie: euro crisis, Grexit debate, refugee crisis, Brexit, and the climate catastrophe, as well as neonationalism, authoritarianism, and populism within and outside the EU. Then the Covid-19 pandemic and the war in Ukraine (and other threats looming). We lurch from one to the next, and each time the chorus of doomsayers gets louder.

One main reason why the EU has survived, at least this far, is that the crises – even if contemporaneous and mutually exacerbating – ultimately proved controllable. No single crisis on its own was severe enough to overwhelm the EU, and although they interacted, they never merged into a storm capable of sinking the ship. Instead, the EU managed to ride successive squalls, often employing means that actually deepened integration in significant areas. Rather than swamping the bridge, past crises brought about largely unnoticed course corrections. There was no grand design and no major reform treaty to give the EU a new direction after the Lisbon Treaty. Attempts to initiate fundamental reform debates did not get very far. Instead, the default was always muddling through.

Today's crises thus play out in dramatically different circumstances. The grim repercussions of economic globalisation cannot be talked away. The international system has been plunged into deep turmoil, along with the political order of many states worldwide, not least through the onslaught of authoritarian populism. Public support for the integration project is often very brittle. Authoritarian populism is a reaction not only to globalisation but also to the EU's historic course of liberalisation. In 2010 former EU Commissioner Mario Monti identified two mutually reinforcing trends exerting increasing pressure on the European project: 'integration fatigue' and 'market fatigue'.[1] And indeed, EU policies were polarised and politicised as never before. European flags flew and burned. It was now clear to all concerned – whether pro or contra – that the Union's economic and social impact was decisive.

There was no single moment when these challenges led the EU to move away from its specific form of liberalisation. But an existing trend has intensified since

---

[1] Mario Monti, *A New Strategy for the Single Market: At the Service of Europe's Economy and Society – Report to the President of the European Commission José Manuel Barroso* (Brussels: EU, 2010) (Document Ares (2016) 841541 – 17/02/2016).

2009, with a very broadly couched concept of security now taking centre stage. This means many things at the same time: mutual survival and safety in an increasingly dangerous and unpredictable world, including the expansion of military capabilities, and preservation of existing institutional achievements. But also a focus on resilient supply chains and material support in times of unforeseen crisis. Overall, people in the member states now tend to be addressed more as citizens than as consumers. Debates about the EU thus tend to gravitate towards 'a Europe that protects' – an expression that French President Emmanuel Macron liked to use and that the Austrian EU Presidency in 2018 even chose as its official motto.[2] The halcyon days of the first two post–Cold War decades, when security concerns became peripheral, are clearly over. The EU's new debate and direction also reflect the loss of the optimism that powered the preceding phase of its history.

Saving the EU from the effects of multiple crises and its own structural instability often meant expanding and deepening its institutional structures – even if those consequences are often overlooked (Figure 5.1). The changes generally occurred informally, without rewriting the treaties. The public debates tend to jump from one crisis narrative to the next, disregarding and underestimating the ways in which the European project has absorbed the onslaught of challenges. As a consequence, the EU has been reaching far beyond its original economic remit. In this time of turmoil, crises were frequently put to productive use – but without ever getting to the roots of the

[2] www.eu2018.at/agenda-priorities/priorities.html (accessed 1 May 2025).

FIGURE 5.1 The heads of the European Council, the European Parliament, and the European Commission – António Costa, David Sassoli, and Ursula von der Leyen – present the Joint Declaration on the Conference on the Future of Europe on 10 March 2021. All are masked on account of the Covid-19 pandemic. The conference was an attempt to come up with a future vision of the EU and to get citizens more involved – to little avail, however. Credit: Getty Images 1231628923.

problems. In other words, the EU was stumbling and often 'failing forward' from one crisis to the next.[3] What we are witnessing today is a third major transformation of the European project, after the foundational decade of the 1950s and the major changes initiated during the 1970s. The third transformation began in the late 2000s in response to the poly-crises confronting the Union. The EU has changed massively, gaining new powers but also becoming more fragile.

---

[3] Erik Jones, R. Daniel Keleman, and Sophie Meunier, 'Failing Forward? The Euro Crisis and the Incomplete Nature of European Integration', *Comparative Political Studies* 49 (2016), pp. 1010–1034.

5 Security First: Course Correction, since 2009

5.1 Uncharted Waters

The euro crisis that erupted in 2009 marked a historical turning point for the integration process. Rather than pursuing grand designs, the EU and its member states were now feeling their way in the dark. From the institutional perspective they weathered the storm astonishingly unscathed, but at the price of creating or aggravating other problems.

The global financial crisis of 2007–2008 laid bare the deficits of the preceding phase of liberalisation at the national, European, and international levels. The collapse began in the United States, where bank deregulation and other liberalisation measures since the 1980s had given financial capitalism a free rein. The heart of the problem was a gigantic property bubble inflated by dubious lending. Other factors exacerbated the situation, such as the US Federal Reserve's policy of cheap money and large capital inflows. The bursting of the subprime bubble triggered a global financial and banking crisis that shook the dominant economic and social model to its core.

In the EU member states the problem initially manifested as a debt crisis (Figure 5.2). As their economies shrank, a growing number of member states struggled to stay within the Maastricht debt criteria, under which their annual budget deficit was not to exceed 3 per cent of GDP and total state debt not more than 60 per cent of GDP. Adding to their woes, many European banks were dragged into the US subprime disaster and required state intervention to avoid bankruptcy. This tore gaping holes in national budgets and sent state debt spiralling,

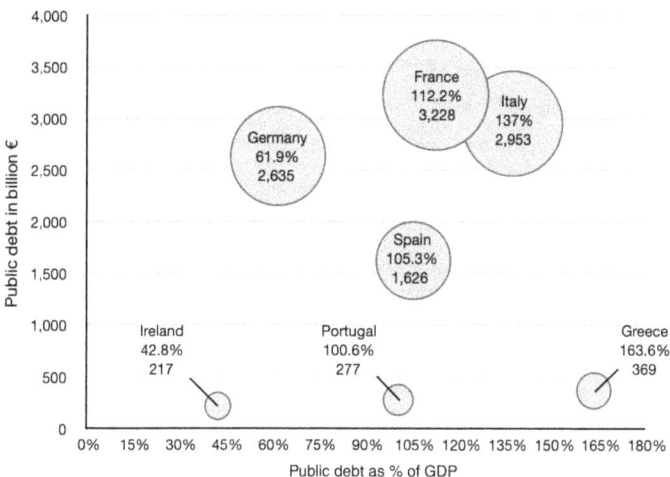

FIGURE 5.2 Public debt and debt-to-GDP in selected EU states, 2010. The absolute amount of debt is much less important than its ratio to GDP. Fortunately for the EU, several of the national economies with highly problematic ratios were rather small, making the rescue efforts easier.

while interest rates spiked in the vulnerable national economies. Greece, Ireland, Italy, Spain, and Portugal faced default on their loan repayments and ultimately state bankruptcy. A more fundamental problem also surfaced now: the far-reaching internationalisation of the deregulated banking and finance sector allowed complications to spread like wildfire from one country to the next. But supranational control of such processes was lacking.

The economic crisis placed Europe's polities under enormous pressure. The Maastricht criteria and other EU policies required governments to impose unpopular austerity measures. Political repercussions were inevitable: across the Eurozone governments collapsed or lost elections: Finland, Greece, Ireland, Italy, Spain, and Portugal in 2011, France, Slovakia, and Slovenia in 2012, and Cyprus and Malta in 2013. In some cases, 'unpolitical' technocrats and experts were put in charge, as in Italy from 2011 to 2013 or the two successive Greek interim cabinets in 2011 and 2012. Crises of government snowballed into crises of democracy; 'Europe', which until 2010 rarely played any significant role in national elections, now triggered a political earthquake across the Eurozone. German Chancellor Angela Merkel's political survival – in changing coalitions – through the entire period represents a notable exception. All this underlines the magnitude of the challenges demanding political answers at the national and European levels.

If that was not enough, the global economic turmoil triggered a euro crisis, which began in 2009 pretty much exactly at the same time as the Treaty of Lisbon came into force. The EU's GDP shrank by more than 4 per cent in 2009, as the vigorous growth of the preceding years evaporated (Figure 5.3). The member states were now facing simultaneous state debt, banking, and financial crises. The problems were so grave that for a time the euro appeared unlikely to survive. This stress test mercilessly exposed the deficits and fragility of the currency structure erected since the 1990s. Now the failure to back up the currency union with measures such as a coordinated financial policy and harmonised banking regulation came back to bite it. The tensions had been visible from the outset, but at that stage there had been no majority for the kind of comprehensive economic integration that would have effectively contained the economic risks.

5.1 Uncharted Waters

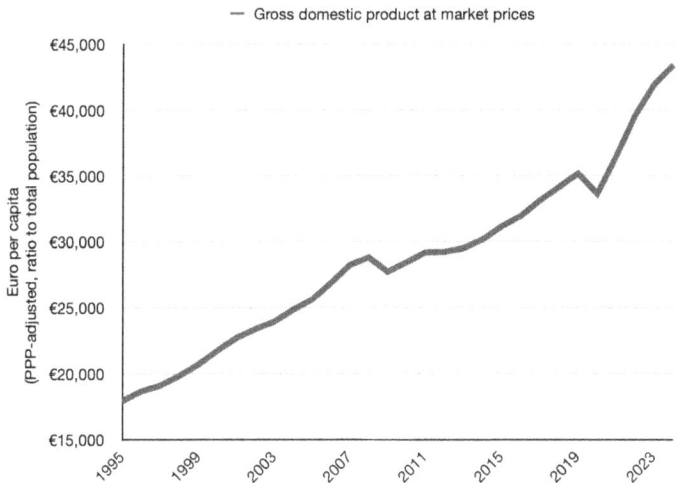

FIGURE 5.3 EU27 real GDP, 1996–2024. The losses during the economic crisis of the late 2000s are very visible. Nobody imagined that roughly a decade later a tiny virus would cause an even more dramatic fall.

Matters came to a head in Greece, where falsified state debt statistics had only disguised the scale of the problems. The cost of bailing out its banks left Greece's Maastricht deficit criteria in tatters. Its credit rating was downgraded to a point where it was no longer able to borrow on the financial markets. In April 2010 Athens was forced to apply for financial aid from Brussels to avoid sovereign default. Within weeks the EU member states created a temporary rescue fund, also to prevent the contagion spreading to other over-indebted member states like Spain and Portugal or even Italy and France. From 2012 the Eurozone states developed this into the permanent European Stability Mechanism (ESM). Cyprus, Greece, Ireland, Portugal, and Spain all had to turn to the safety net provided by the ESM and other schemes.

5 Security First: Course Correction, since 2009

The problems with Greece kept the fate of the euro hanging in the balance for quite some time. The idea of the country withdrawing from the common currency – soon labelled 'Grexit' – was understood not as an act of Greek national liberation but a way to save the euro from Greece's problems repaying its debts and complying with the terms of the aid. The crisis came to a head in 2014–2015, when immense efforts on all sides were required to keep the country in the euro.

The price of avoiding 'Grexit' was immense – for Greece and other states under austerity measures, and for the EU as a whole: the crisis took not just the euro but the entire integration process to the brink of implosion. And it stripped the EU of the aura of dynamism and optimism it had acquired in the 1990s.

Politicians were operating under enormous pressure during this entire phase. Improvisation was the order of the day, rather than fundamental reforms, and the prospect of catastrophic failure inspired a great deal of institutional innovation. This had consequences for the distribution of power between the various organs. The heads of state and government frequently had to intervene in person to save the day. The Commission, the European Parliament, and the national parliaments tended to be sidelined, even if Jean-Claude Juncker's Commission in particular regarded itself as a political actor. Certain aspects such as the ESM were institutionally and legally separate from the EU, strengthening the role of the member states' governments (Box 5.1). As so often in this labyrinthine system, there was also a countervailing supranational trend, albeit much less pronounced. Concretely, the European Central Bank secured an expanded role. This was seen especially in

5.1 Uncharted Waters

> **Box 5.1** European Stability Mechanism
>
> The ESM was established in 2012 as an intergovernmental organisation located in Luxembourg. It was designed to be independent of the EU and the Eurozone, operating under public international law for all Eurozone member states that had ratified the ESM treaty. During the Eurozone crisis it served as a firewall and arranged immediate financial assistance for member states in need. It replaced two earlier EU funding schemes established in 2010. The ESM represents a shift away from supranational government and strengthened the intergovernmental side of the EU in a time of crisis. In December 2012, Spain was the first country to receive disbursements from the ESM to recapitalise its ailing banks. Others followed. During the Covid-19 pandemic the ESM opened a credit line to help Eurozone member states deal with the economic and social consequences.

2012 when its President Mario Draghi told the nervous financial markets on 26 July that the ECB was 'ready to do whatever it takes to preserve the euro'.[4] The impact of that impromptu statement was enormous. It brought the rampant speculation against the euro to an abrupt halt. Draghi's 'whatever it takes' made history and marked, with hindsight, the turning point of the escalating euro crisis. The EU's economic situation gradually stabilised. Instead of EU-style liberalisation, financial stability and new pillars to secure existing achievements moved to the fore.

---

[4] 'Speech by Mario Draghi, President of the European Central Bank, at the Global Investment Conference in London, 26 July 2012', ECB website, www.ecb.europa.eu/press/key/date/2012/html/sp120726.en.html (accessed 1 May 2025).

Three objectives were prioritised in response to the euro crisis: preserving financial capitalism as the basis of the economies of the member states; consolidating their national budgets; and securing the institutional achievements of the EU and the Eurozone. The political and economic elites of the member states never doubted that the euro must be preserved. As German Chancellor Angela Merkel put it in September 2011, 'If the euro fails, Europe fails.'[5] This explains both the national measures to support the banks and the European rescue packages. There were other new instruments too, especially stricter monitoring of national budgets, stronger regulation of the European financial markets, and a banking union with closer banking oversight. Most of the institutional changes came in the turbulent years between 2010 and 2013, although in some cases the 'rescue packages' for individual countries ran longer. The European Fiscal Compact adopted in 2012 heavily curbed national policy options. Now any country failing to meet the Maastricht convergence criteria had to reckon with painful financial sanctions.

Measures with innocuous-sounding names like budgetary consolidation, Six-Pack (for six measures adopted in 2011 to reform the Stability and Growth Pact), and European Semester wreaked social devastation in the member states. The neoliberal spirit of many of the measures played an important role. For example, in return for financial assistance Greece had to submit to a brutal

---

[5] 'Merkel: "If the Euro Fails, Europe Fails"', *BBC News*, 7 September 2011, www.bbc.com/news/av/business-14827834 (accessed 1 May 2025).

austerity regime of spending cuts and privatisations overseen by the 'troika' of the ECB, European Commission, and International Monetary Fund. The term 'troika' became so toxic that in 2015 the Greek government asked for it to be replaced with 'institutions' in official communications. Never before had a member state experienced such dramatic negative effects of EU membership in such a short space of time. Many Greeks found themselves plunged into poverty. In the short and medium term austerity policies exacerbated the crisis, especially spending-slashing technocratic budgets without direct democratic legitimation. Mass unemployment was one of the gravest consequences, with youth unemployment exceeding 50 per cent at times. The harshness of the measures inflicted on ordinary people stood in stark contrast to the generosity received by the banks. Especially in the southern member states this generated great frustration and bitterness.

Social distress almost inevitably produced political turmoil. Most of the mainstream parties backed the austerity course, if with gritted teeth; in this respect a ruling consensus existed. The chosen approach – concentrating on 'bigger issues' rather than ordinary people – triggered resistance. In summer 2016 Greek Finance Minister Yanis Varoufakis made international headlines with his opposition to the troika's austerity policy. Little was achieved, and the course of events was grist to the mill of extremist currents. And it was no longer possible to ignore the narrow limits the EU placed on national sovereignty and parliaments. Although left-wing populism benefited for a time, for example in Greece and Spain, right-wing populism was the bigger winner.

The European option was increasingly contested and controversial. EU flags burned in Athens and elsewhere, with particular vitriol directed towards Angela Merkel and the German government, which was seen as the enforcer of austerity. The response to the Eurozone crisis was a massive deepening of integration. It cemented the iron cage of capitalism and technocratic efficiency without heed to the wishes of ordinary people.

Behind all the drama and protest, it was easy to overlook the double paradox involved. Containing Germany's economic strength was one of the original and central motivations for creating the euro in the first place. And now the common currency had become a stick to beat any nation stepping out of line with Berlin's political preferences and an orthodox reading of the *acquis communautaire*. Together with other stability-oriented states such as the Netherlands, the German government insisted on preserving and protecting the existing system. The priority was to save the underlying structure through austerity and a certain deepening of integration. And a policy established to check German power now turned into an instrument controlled by Berlin – at least at first glance.

The second paradox was even less obvious. The stronger the turn to austerity, the more the Maastricht criteria were undermined. The debt 'communitisation' demanded by the net recipients encountered bitter resistance from the net contributors: European integration hardly budged on that axis. At the time such a course was unthinkable in the prosperous northern nations, where discussions frequently revolved around the supposed indolence and profligacy of the southern Europeans. At the same time significant funds were suddenly being provided by countries that had previously been telling their own populations that the coffers were empty. So, it would be wrong to simply dismiss the measures as neoliberal. The ECB's massive purchases of sovereign bonds and the establishment of a permanent ESM subverted the no-bailout clause of 1992, under which member states (and the EU as a whole) could not be held liable for other member states' commitments. Gradually, the course edged away from the monetary slant upon which Germany and its allies had originally insisted, and the ECB acquired an explicitly political role. It was no coincidence that the President of the German Bundesbank, Jens Weidmann – who opposed this policy – knew nothing about Draghi's 2012 statement in advance. Despite (or precisely because of) its increasingly political role, the EU experienced a barrage of criticism from all sides, directed towards specific measures and the organisation as a whole. The crisis of the economy thus led to a crisis of confidence that knocked liberalisation off its perch.

Greek pensioners like Stelios Vitzilaios, who had worked since the age of fourteen for a pre-crisis pension of €650 that was now cut by €100, could not care less about such paradoxes.[6] They had other, more existential worries. But for the EU's overall structure this surreptitious reorientation of monetary policy amounted to an important transformation. Despite austerity, a new level of communitisation had been attained.

The euro crisis also revealed just how far European integration had progressed – and for precisely that reason

---

[6] Lefteris Papadimas, 'Thousands of Greek Pensioners Protest against Cuts as More Austerity Looms', *Reuters*, 4 April 2017.

5 Security First: Course Correction, since 2009

divided the member states. It was now much clearer than in the founding phase that the common currency had transformed state sovereignty and left national governments with scant leeway of their own. 'Europe' faced governments and populations with tough choices. The EU's rules produced winners and losers. For example, the structure of the euro meant that Greece had no recourse to the classical instrument of currency devaluation. Yet Germany, which was much less badly affected, actually profited from the crisis. On account of its perceived stability the German state was able to borrow at negative interest rates. And as a comparison between Estonia and Greece demonstrates, Europeanisation did not automatically produce homogenisation: while Estonia's per capita GDP almost doubled between 2010 and 2019, from €11,000 to €21,000, Greece's fell from €20,000 to €17,000.

Integration forced the euro countries into a collective straitjacket while driving them apart. With the price of abandoning the project apparently exorbitant, they instead pursued closer integration. Never before had the EU mobilised such enormous material and institutional resources to bail out entire economies. But they stopped short of the debt communitisation demanded by Athens, Madrid, Paris, and Rome. The compromise was the path of least resistance, the minimum required to keep the euro alive. While this approach still bore the hallmarks of neoliberalism, the pressure for opening was less forceful than in the two preceding decades.

Developments in the sphere of migration and asylum reflect a quite different approach to dealing with inadequacies. Here again, it was the confrontation with

5.1 Uncharted Waters

extraneous crisis that exposed weaknesses in the EU's existing arrangements. Yet again the member states and the EU as a whole were flying blind, but this time they were unable to agree on solutions based on deepening. Instead, priority was given to defending the existing status quo and sealing the borders.

This crisis culminated in 2015 when more than one million informal migrants and refugees arrived in the EU. Their reasons were diverse, with most originating from impoverished and war-torn regions of the Middle East and Africa; the largest national group came from Syria. The term used at the time, 'refugee crisis', tended to locate the problem in the migrants themselves, rather than in the inadequacy of political responses to the challenges. And indeed, many of the actions taken by the EU and its member states were designed to reduce the numbers of people arriving rather than to address the causes of migration or to iron out inconsistencies in its own rules. Experts had in fact been circulating such demands for quite some time. Essentially all that happened in 2015 was that an existing problem became too visible to ignore.

The possibilities for refugees and asylum seekers to enter and remain in the EU had been shrinking for decades. The Union's doors were now firmly closed to most labour migrants from the Global South. Even in 2015 many attempts to enter the EU ended in failure; for some the outcome was fatal. In September 2015 the image of the body of two-year-old Alan Kurdi shocked the world. The Syrian Kurdish family had already made two unsuccessful attempts to reach the EU. They tried again in the early morning of 2 September, setting off from the Turkish coast in a rubber dinghy. They hoped to

5 Security First: Course Correction, since 2009

reach the Greek island of Kos just four kilometres away. Alan drowned. His five-year-old brother Galip drowned. Their mother Rehan drowned. Only their father Abdullah survived. The photograph of Alan's corpse washed up on a Turkish beach shocked Europe and the world. The family's fate stands for the many thousands whose deaths went unreported, for whom Europe offered no refuge.

Even those who did reach the EU faced enormous challenges. The situation spotlighted all the problems and deficits of European integration in this area. 'Processing' of arrivals was at times extremely chaotic. The rules were tightened to make it harder to acquire refugee status. The humanitarian catastrophe cast a cynical light on the idea of the EU as a community of values. Under the Dublin rules introduced in the 1990s the country where a migrant first entered the EU was responsible for their asylum process. In practice this placed the greatest burden on Mediterranean states whose capacities were already stretched to breaking point. But their calls for a fairer system fell on deaf ears. In this way, the internal imbalances increased the pressure on the member states and on the EU as a whole.

The situation came to a head in 2015. Since the spring increasing numbers of people had been entering the EU via the eastern Mediterranean, almost all of them from Turkey to Greece (often passing through non-EU Balkan states en route to Hungary and Croatia). Many hoped to move on rapidly to the United Kingdom, Germany, or Scandinavia. The Greek state, still mired in the aftermath of the euro crisis, was overwhelmed and largely permitted them to do so. Meanwhile, the situation in the camps, for instance at Idomeni on the Greek-North Macedonian

5.1 Uncharted Waters

border, became increasingly unbearable. The Italian government and others facilitated onward movement. Soon hundreds of thousands without regular immigration documents were heading northwards.

The magnitude of the trek initially steamrollered the Dublin rules and the Schengen system. Many member states responded unilaterally. For a time the external border became extremely porous in places, while national borders within the EU were enforced again. Both developments violated the spirit – and in some cases the letter – of Dublin and Schengen. And measures were frequently imposed without coordination with other member states. That applied not only to decisions to close national borders but also to responses to the humanitarian drama, for example when the German and Austrian governments decided in the night from 4 to 5 September 2015 to open their borders to refugees who were already in the EU. This lack of coordination weakened the EU and further undermined its rules.

The sequence of events had wider repercussions too. Schengen was no longer the emblem of an open Europe. Now 'illegal' migrants 'flooding' into the EU dominated the media reporting, border posts were reactivated – and resistance to the restrictions re-emerged (Figure 5.4). The more porous the hard external borders became, the more visible the hitherto almost invisible internal frontiers appeared.

Another factor also pushed Schengen towards greater emphasis on security. Islamist terrorist attacks, most prominently in Paris in November 2015 and in Brussels in March 2016, also led to tighter border controls within the Schengen area. And so the changes affected not only

5 Security First: Course Correction, since 2009

FIGURE 5.4 Drawing by Lebanese–Swiss cartoonist Patrick Chappatte, published in a Swiss newspaper, 6 March 2020. Credit: Chappatte in *Le Temps*, Geneva.

extremists and asylum seekers but also businesses, tourists, and cross-border commuters.

The ensuing debate also created deep rifts within an EU that found itself overwhelmed at the practical level by the challenges of asylum, migration, and borders. On the one side there was unprecedented solidarity with people in need and concerted public and civil society efforts to help them – and on the other the rise of nationalist, authoritarian, and frequently racist populism. Between the two poles many were left wondering whether their society could afford the assistance, and yet again why resources were suddenly so readily available when they had been told for so long that there was nothing to spare.

Unlike the euro crisis, the toxic debate over migration left no plausible opening for initiatives to overcome the crisis by deepening integration. This was not for lack of proposals. In 2015, for instance, the Commission put forward a system for distributing migrants among the member states. But few such ideas made it into practice. The differences between governments remained unbridgeable and – unlike the euro crisis – the refugee crisis did not lead to greater European integration. No strong centralised institution emerged at the institutional level (unlike for example the ECB for the common currency). The exception that proves the rule is the border agency Frontex, whose mandate, budget, and staff expanded substantially after 2015.

Beyond this rather technical point, there was no consensus about what the challenge actually was. Many countries saw little need for reform, because their geographical location and the existing system absolved them of most of the burden. On the other side, those receiving the largest numbers of asylum seekers, first and foremost the Mediterranean nations, pressed hardest for reforms. At the same time the debates were frequently centred on the nation and national interests rather than the EU as a whole or the needs of those affected. In the face of all these conflicts, reverting to the – slightly tweaked – status quo ante turned out to be the path of least resistance. The EU did not entirely bend before the pressure of authoritarian populism, but it did step up efforts to fortify its external borders.

Securing the existing meant above all reducing the external pressure, in some respects by legally and ethically questionable means. In the end negotiations in 2015–2016 with Turkey, as the main point of entry at the time, significantly reduced the problem for the European Union. In return for billions of euros in aid Turkey agreed to take back anyone who entered Greece illegally, and above all to prevent further crossings into the EU. The deal, which basically relocated the problem outside the European Union, was only partially implemented. Nevertheless, from 2016 the numbers of people trying to enter the EU illegally fell significantly. Other countries, especially in North Africa, also received billions of euros to police, hold, and return refugees. The situation for migrants was often catastrophic, but the EU externalised the problem and the responsibility for its consequences. Now the EU was focusing less on improving its management of migration and asylum, more on deterring migration and 'securitising' its external borders – a word quite as ugly as the reality it describes.

All this weakened the EU politically. The growing role of groups such as the anti-reformist Visegrád states (Czech Republic, Hungary, Poland, and Slovakia) highlighted internal divisions, as did the unilateral decisions of Germany and Sweden in the so-called refugee crisis. The deal with Turkey made the EU beholden to a third state that was exhibiting increasingly authoritarian traits at the time. The idea of 'A Europe that protects' was increasingly understood as a Europe that protects *itself*.

5.2 Closing and Bolting the Door

In March 2010 an Icelandic volcano with an unpronounceable name erupted violently. The ash in the atmosphere caused the cancellation of more than one hundred thousand flights within and across Europe in April. The eruption of Eyjafjallajökull was just the first of a whole string of crises over the course of more than a decade.

5.2 Closing and Bolting the Door

Voters, values, and viruses topped the bill. War followed. Despite these immense challenges, unity prevailed over division and the EU concentrated more than ever on securing its achievements and asserting its role.

This is seen most clearly in the Brexit story. With his referendum on British membership, Prime Minister David Cameron hoped to clarify the question once and for all and take the wind out of the sails of the anti-EU UKIP (United Kingdom Independence Party). On 23 June 2016 the British electorate voted to leave by a narrow majority of 52 to 48 per cent. The outcome surprised even many Brexiteers and was certainly a shock for the other European capitals, whose mantra had been demolished. Now, undeniably, enlargement and deepening were not the only possible directions of travel (if occasionally paused for brief crises). Until 2016 this had been treated as an iron rule – even if the departures of Algeria in 1962 and Greenland in 1985 remind us that it has never actually been an 'ever growing union'.

The Brexit negotiations were long and tortuous, revealing just how difficult it had become to leave the EU. Since the transformation phase of the 1980s the integration process had deepened to a point where a quick sharp break had become technically impossible and politically explosive. The arduous Brexit talks exposed the depth of division in British society, widened the rifts between the camps, and plunged the country into deep crisis, while the prospect of leaving the EU fanned secessionist currents especially in Scotland and Northern Ireland. Several prime ministers fell in quick succession, while parliament and the highest courts faced unprecedented criticism. Trumpeted as restoring the nation's sovereignty, Brexit boomeranged to threaten the very survival of the United Kingdom.

The rest of the EU passed the Brexit test a great deal better than expected. Losing the economic and political weight of the United Kingdom naturally weakened the Union, and it failed to come up with any clear vision or counternarrative. But it did succeed in speaking with a single voice to a degree that surprised many observers. London's attempts to sow discord came to naught, largely because governments in Dublin, Madrid, Rome, Vilnius, and elsewhere feared that a good deal for the British would boost centrifugal tendencies in other quarters. The historic core project, the Single Market, turned out to be surprisingly robust and the EU successfully defended its status quo and integrity. While it might appear paradoxical, the EU navigated the Brexit process astonishingly successfully. A national trauma for the British, Brexit was just one of many crises for the EU – and one it coped with comparably well.

In this context unity became the new mantra. The euro crisis had boosted populist currents across Europe, especially those of an authoritarian and nationalist bent. Until 2016 Marine Le Pen in France, Geert Wilders in the Netherlands, the Freedom Party in Austria, and others argued more or less openly for their country to leave the EU. Support for that option from Vladimir Putin and soon also Donald Trump increased the external pressure but also provoked push-back. Many of those who criticised the EU now shied away from advocating withdrawal. And as the Brexit trouble dragged on, exit discussions all but vanished in the remaining EU states. That is unlikely to change as long as Brexit appears to present more and

5.2 Closing and Bolting the Door

bigger problems for the United Kingdom than for the EU. As long as Brexit is the point of reference, the exit option will inevitably appear negative.

Brexit has done nothing to defuse the conflicts within the EU, however. The stakes are high and the big guns are out. Growing social polarisation within the member states since the 2000s has increasingly been reproduced at the European level. As in other parts of the world, a dichotomy between authoritarian/ethnocentric and liberal/cosmopolitan currents has supplanted the traditional left/right understanding of politics. Criticism of economic globalisation – long a preserve of the left – has increasingly been co-opted by the authoritarian/ethnocentric camp, which also adopted a generally negative stance towards the EU. In the May 2014 European elections, right-wing EU-critical parties gained almost 20 per cent of MEPs; together with other Eurosceptic parties their share was nearly 30 per cent or about 10 percentage points more than in the previous election. This shift to the right has continued, and the EU has found itself challenged from within its own parliament as never before.

Another, possibly even bigger danger is less visible. Those most critical of the EU were now discussing subverting and restructuring it, rather than leaving. Hungarian Prime Minister Viktor Orbán and his 'illiberal democracy' is the most prominent example: a government originally formed through largely free and fair elections sets about dismantling rule of law and minority protections and weakening the independent media; it rejects pluralism for a model based on supposedly traditional ideas about Christianity, gender relations, and the nation. Ideas of this ilk have gained ground across Europe, most of all in Poland and Slovakia, where they were able to define state policies at least for a time.

This reorientation played out primarily at the level of the nation state but had important implications for the EU too. While the authoritarian populists (thus far) lacked the strength to push through fundamental changes at the European level, they have certainly succeeded in influencing asylum and migration policies and blocking a stronger orientation on values. Moreover, they have stepped up their efforts to cooperate transnationally, both within the EU and with (far) right movements in the United States and elsewhere. Some have accepted support from Putin's Russia. Such cooperation seems paradoxical, since all these groups claim to put the interests of their own nation first. That is why such alliances have always been fragile and internally fractious. At the same time, all these groups present themselves as the saviours of the 'true' Europe.

The EU has been largely powerless to prevent this. The issue came to a head over a controversial judicial reform in Poland, which according to the European Commission and the European Parliament jeopardised the rule of law and EU values. At the end of 2017 the Juncker Commission initiated the 'Article 7' disciplinary process for the first time since it was introduced under the Treaty of Lisbon. This represented a further sign that the Commission saw itself as a political actor, not just the guardian of the treaties. Warsaw conceded, but not an inch more than necessary. Since the late 2010s the European institutions have also increasingly employed their instruments against Hungary in order

5.2 Closing and Bolting the Door

to secure democracy and rule of law, again with rather meagre results. The mechanisms for securing norms and values within the EU remained unsatisfactory and drew sharp criticism from those who saw the EU as a guarantor of values and baulked at their taxes funding states with illiberal and increasingly authoritarian traits. And these were only the most obvious instances where the EU failed to live up to its own promises. The gap between aspiration and actuality grew ever wider. Poland did not return to an EU-compliant course until the Law and Justice Party (PiS) was voted out of office in 2023 and Donald Tusk returned as prime minister. However, the structural problem of challenges within the EU as a whole remained. Moreover, politics has become ever more volatile, with growing electoral support for politically fundamentally different and often incompatible positions. For a political entity premised on continuity, compromise, and incremental change, as is the EU, this poses a fundamental challenge.

All these problems point to a fundamental deficit. The EU possesses extensive mechanisms for monitoring the accession process and has generally been quite successful in sanctioning member states' violations in the economic sphere, as the original core of European integration. The situation is considerably trickier with violations of democracy and rule of law, which remain a good deal less clearly codified in the *acquis communautaire*. Decisions adopted at the end of 2020 – against Polish and Hungarian resistance – might do something to address this issue, but values will remain a quandary for the EU.

Alongside the EU institutions, civil society has also taken up the challenge of authoritarian populism. Citizens

5 Security First: Course Correction, since 2009

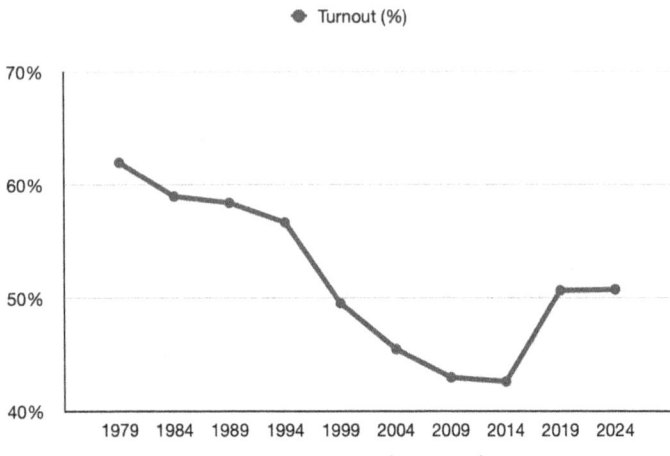

FIGURE 5.5 Turnout at European Parliament elections since 1979.

themselves have rallied to the EU in response to its own crises and in opposition to the global growth of authoritarian tendencies – from Brazil to India, Russia to the Philippines, the United States to Turkey. Turnout at the 2019 European elections was the highest in twenty years – after a continuous decline since the first direct election in 1979. It was topped by a few tenths of a per cent in 2024 (Figure 5.5). And while growth in support for EU-critical parties stalled in 2019, their gains in 2024 were substantial. Civil society mobilised new forces across the political spectrum. The more people became aware of the stakes, the more they took to the streets for and against the EU. None of this was fundamentally new, but the polarisation fostered a new political dynamic that now shapes the integration process.

Whether such initiatives lead to sustained mobilisation or even new institutional forms of participation remains to be seen. The aforementioned Conference on the Future of Europe (2020–2022), which attempted to

5.2 Closing and Bolting the Door

involve citizens in the debate about EU reform, passed off largely unnoticed and produced no lasting results. Those who did follow the debates often felt they were witnessing yet another poorly executed attempt to rally support for the Union through a technocratic initiative from above. Recent European elections also illustrate how whipping up exaggerated hopes or fears can deepen disappointment. Despite its rather shaky legal basis, there were great expectations that the *Spitzenkandidat* process would lend the EU greater democratic legitimacy. (The *Spitzenkandidat* process was introduced under the Lisbon Treaty and first applied in the 2014 European elections. Under it the European parties each select a lead candidate for the European Parliament election; in theory the *Spitzenkandidat* from the winning party becomes the President of the European Commission.) But the heads of state and government did not feel bound by the arrangement, and in a typical act of back-room politicking appointed Ursula von der Leyen as President of the European Commission in 2019. Welcome as it is to see a woman heading the Commission for the first time, the wheeler-dealing in Brussels left many disillusioned. Von der Leyen's re-election in 2024 did not amount to a clear commitment to the *Spitzenkandidat* model either.

Internal rifts eroded the EU's external attraction. Croatia did join as the twenty-eighth member state in 2013 – leaving the European Union back at twenty-seven members after Brexit. Talks with Turkey and other (potential) accession candidates in the Western Balkans continued. But neither side placed much hope in the talks during the 2010s, as the EU experienced 'enlargement fatigue'. Relations with Istanbul suffered at the time, with Turkey increasingly operating as an autonomous regional power. Iceland applied for membership in 2009 but officially withdrew its application in 2015; Switzerland's relationship with the EU has cooled markedly. As the idealism drained from the European project, the global rise of (neo-)nationalism, the crisis of multilateralism, and the new role of China eclipsed the EU's regional integration paradigm. Here again the question was preserving the existing and securing a modicum of capacity, rather than great hopes and grand designs. The universalist aspirations of the integration process, which had gained traction since the 1980s, now weakened again. During the 2010s, the EU lost much of its regional and global attractiveness, which in turn reinforced its reorientation towards security matters.

The distractions of dealing with internal problems hindered the development of the European Foreign and Security Policy and closer relations with countries in the immediate neighbourhood, at least until 2022. Certain institutional reforms were carried through, such as creating the High Representative of the Union for Foreign Affairs and Security Policy in 2009, on the basis of the Treaty of Lisbon. But such organisational changes did not translate directly into tangible politics. When the 'Arab spring' erupted in late 2010 and a string of nations in North Africa and the Middle East rose up against authoritarian rulers, the EU long lacked a meaningful position. Brussels made grand statements – such as 'We want to be Tunisia's strongest ally in their move towards democracy' – but there was little concrete follow-up and above all little fundamentally new at this critical juncture.[7] In 2011 the European Union found itself divided over the question of international military intervention in Libya and was more or less unable to influence the conflict in its own name. Given the complexity of the issues that is perhaps unsurprising. But measured against the ambition of a viable community of values pursuing an effective foreign and neighbourhood policy, it certainly fell short. Instead of supporting pro-democracy movements, the EU – especially from 2015 – focused first on protecting its own interests. Here again, *realpolitik* outpaced universalist aspirations.

And where the EU did adopt a clear stance in the early 2010s, it tended to overestimate its role. This was particularly true for Ukraine. Its entrenched self-image as an irresistible magnet for states in its neighbourhood now contributed to a major international crisis. When Brussels negotiated an association agreement with Kyiv between 2012 and 2014 it demonstrated little awareness of the geopolitical sensitivity of the situation in face of an increasingly aggressive Russian foreign policy under Vladimir Putin. The conflict escalated in 2013–2014 when the pro-Russian President Viktor Yanukovych refused under Russian pressure to sign the negotiated agreement. Hundreds of thousands took to the streets in support of the agreement and further-reaching demands. Yanukovych was removed from office and fled to Russia. The conflict spiralled completely out of control when Putin destabilised Ukraine by annexing Crimea in March

---

[7] https://ec.europa.eu/commission/presscorner/detail/de/SPEECH_11_101 (accessed 1 May 2025).

2014 and igniting a military conflict in eastern Ukraine a few weeks later. The European Union utterly failed to anticipate these developments, nor was it able to respond clearly and coherently when faced with Russian aggression on its doorstep. Geopolitically it remained a dwarf.

The military spending data illustrates the EU's weakness in this dimension. In 2019 the EU countries (minus the United Kingdom) accounted for about 12 per cent of global military spending, far behind the United States (39 per cent) but ahead of China (10 per cent) and clearly ahead of Russia (less than 4 per cent). So, Europe certainly possesses military might. But the EU – as distinct from individual member states – struggled to project military power on the global stage; very often during the 2010s there was simply no shared European position on security issues. It was punching far below its weight, failing to live up to its own expectations. Proliferating global challenges now demanded an ever-growing role.

The start of a fully fledged war in Ukraine following the Russian invasion on 24 February 2022 was a major turning point for the EU. It exhibited almost unprecedented unity, responding quickly to provide civilian and military support. Employing its policies creatively, it was no longer just the member states and NATO that acted. The EU itself also came up with meaningful responses. European leaders travelled regularly to Kyiv and other parts of the war-torn country to demonstrate their solidarity. Several million people (mainly women and children) were given temporary protection with little bureaucracy; many billions of euros flowed into Ukraine to stabilise and rebuild the country. Alongside individual member states, the EU itself financed arms deliveries on an unprecedented scale; the European Peace Facility (EPF), which was only created in 2021, played a decisive role at the institutional level. At the same time, the EU agreed more than a dozen sanctions packages against the Russian Federation. Along with NATO, the EU also gained new appeal, as reflected in the applications for membership submitted by Ukraine, Moldova, and Georgia within weeks of the Russian invasion.

As unexpected and remarkable as these changes were, and whatever new hopes there may now be that the EU could contribute to peace by facing down Russian aggression, what has been achieved falls well short of expectations and geopolitical needs. The EU's support has not given Ukraine a decisive advantage; US backing was indispensable. As always, new EU policies and instruments continued to develop incrementally. Beyond the immediate consequences for the war in Ukraine, all this only reinforced the EU's shift towards security, which had begun years earlier. Against the scale of the new challenges, the EU's options remained fairly limited, despite instruments such as the EPF and a massive rise in the member states' defence spending since 2022.

These problems were exacerbated by the growing transatlantic rift. During his first presidency from 2017 to 2021, Donald Trump was scathing about the EU and supported Brexit. He declared war on multilateralism, disparaged free trade in general, and questioned the relevance of NATO. Tension rather than cooperation characterised his attitude towards the EU, just as trade mutated from a transatlantic bridge into a field of conflict. Instead of liberalisation, punitive tariffs and retaliatory measures were the order of the day, boosting protectionism

5 Security First: Course Correction, since 2009

on both sides. On top of this came discord over central global strategic issues, such as the nuclear agreement with Iran, where the EU played an unusually important role in the negotiations between 2003 and 2015. The otherwise so low-key Angela Merkel spoke for many when she said after Trump's bizarre performances at the NATO and G7 Summits in May 2017: 'We Europeans must take our fate into our own hands.'[8] Important words, even if the action that followed fell far short of their implications.

The pressure was strongest in the sphere of security, first and foremost in the face of Russian aggression, but also in relation to the reignited Middle East conflict and growing tensions with China. And seeing some of its members, such as the British and Polish, falling in behind Trump on important issues made the EU's situation no easier: another deep rift within. Brexit also weakened the EU geostrategically, and especially militarily. There had already been a debate about whether NATO had become superfluous in the 1990s; the organisation came under even greater pressure in the Trump years. With or without the caprices of its 45th president, America's global power was waning and even a close alliance would no longer have protected the EU and its member states as it had during the Cold War decades. Realisation that the security cocoon in which the EU had originally flourished was

---

[8] 'Merkel: "We Europeans Must Take Our Fate into Our Own Hands"', *Irish Times*, 29 May 2017, www.irishtimes.com/news/world/europe/merkel-we-europeans-must-take-our-fate-into-our-own-hands-1.3100032; for the German original, see for example, 'Wir Europäer müssen unser Schicksal in unsere eigene Hand nehmen', *Handelsblatt*, 28 May 2017, www.handelsblatt.com/politik/deutschland/angela-merkel-wir-europaeer-muessen-unser-schicksal-in-unsere-eigene-hand-nehmen/19861340.html (both accessed 1 May 2025).

5.2 Closing and Bolting the Door

gone forever spurred discussions about massively expanding the EU's own capacities in this sphere. In terms of action, though, the policy of gradualism continued, with the EU increasingly underlining its desire for 'strategic autonomy' (Box 5.2). But there was no real breakthrough, the member states' interests, resources, and approaches were too disparate.

All these problems were exacerbated when Trump returned to power in 2025. While his basic positions remained unchanged, he was better prepared to realise them this time round. His politics are rooted in his disdain for multilateralism, reliability, and compromise, with serious consequences for the EU–US relationship. Erraticism characterises his actions. At the time of writing, only two things are clear. Firstly, Europe, and the EU, can no longer rely on the transatlantic partnership, and especially the security guarantee. And secondly, it will be extremely difficult for the continent and its institutions to rise to the coming geopolitical and military challenges.

Box 5.2 Strategic autonomy

A concept with a longer prehistory at the national level within the EU, especially in France. In the EU context the notion has antecedents in the Franco-British Saint Malo Declaration of 1998 in which French President Jacques Chirac and British Prime Minister Tony Blair agreed that the EU 'must have the capacity for autonomous decision-making and action, backed up by credible military forces ... in order to respond to international crises'. They were responding to the armed conflict in Kosovo in the late 1990s, another intra-European conflict where the

EU failed to play a meaningful role. At that juncture the debate was focused on security policy and international relations. Strategic autonomy became an official objective for the EU in the 2016 EU Global Strategy document, which stressed the need to improve the Union's defence capabilities. Over time the meaning of the term expanded to include other issues such as the economy and the capacity to uphold democratic values. The debate has largely been shaped by shifting external challenges to European integration, such as the Trump presidencies, the Covid-19 pandemic after 2020, and Russia's invasion of Ukraine in 2022. The French government has been particularly active in pushing the concept, which has gained considerable traction among experts, even if some prefer alternative terms such as (strategic) sovereignty. While some argue that the concept has become the EU's new catchphrase, its substance remains vague and enthusiasm is weaker in countries with a more transatlantic tradition. Nevertheless, the debate is evidence of a new urge to think about the EU's role more strategically and to make its policies more assertive. The discussion also reflects the pivot away from EU-style liberalisation.

So, the EU remained weak in the sphere of security, but an economic giant, the world's largest trading bloc. In a global climate characterised by nationalism, populism, and increasingly protectionism, it held fast to multilateralism and international trade. Doing so was much more difficult than it used to be, not just because of the shift in US policies. The World Trade Organization (WTO; successor to the GATT since 1995), as the world's largest international economic organisation, soon became dysfunctional. The Doha Round of negotiations, launched in 2001, tried to combine trade

5.2 Closing and Bolting the Door

liberalisation with new rules but progress stalled very quickly. Instead of contributing to global negotiations under the banner of the WTO, the EU has therefore shifted its emphasis. It concluded and renewed bilateral trade agreements, for example with Canada (2017), Mexico (2018), and Japan (2019), although the deal with Canada was nearly overturned at the ratification stage after objections from a regional parliament in a single member state. Under pressure of public criticism, the national parliaments were granted a greater say in trade policy, which had long been the sole prerogative of the EU. Many of the complaints were well justified and reflected public resistance to liberalisation and neoliberalism. The same can be said of the years of negotiations for a free trade agreement with the United States, which drew massive protest even before it was dropped by Trump in his first term. The heightened politicisation of trade constrained the EU in the global arena but also opened new doors.

Trade between the United States and the EU grew massively in the first twenty years of the new century, but after 2008 the US and European financial sectors began to grow apart. China became increasingly important for every world region, the EU no exception, but tensions between the West and China were also on the rise. The tide of globalisation was turning, with less priority on free trade and global interconnections. Now regulatory initiatives and international politics sought to protect economies rather than promote trade. Globalisation came in for great political criticism. There are serious indications that it has passed its peak as an economic process and that it has been stagnating since the global financial crisis of

5 Security First: Course Correction, since 2009

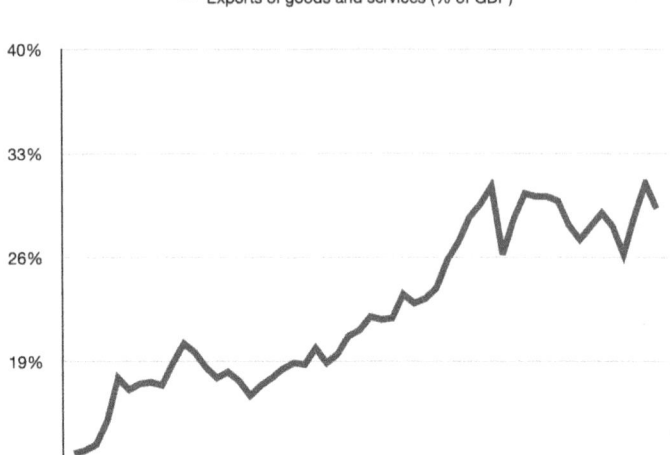

FIGURE 5.6 Ratio of world goods exports to GDP since the 1970s. According to this indicator the 2010s and 2020s are a period of stagnating globalisation.

the late 2000s. According to some indicators it is even regressing (Figure 5.6). US tariff policies during Trump's second term are reinforcing retrenchment.

This trend was reinforced by another dynamic. The EU had already overtaken the United States as the leading environmental regulator in the course of the 1990s, and this development continued in the 2010s. It was most visible in relation to the Paris Climate Agreement, which the EU backed vigorously. President Trump withdrew the United States from the agreement, doing lasting harm to its reputation; his successor Joe Biden reversed the decision immediately on taking office. On the first day of his second term, Trump withdrew again. While Washington prevaricated, the EU raised its sights at the end of 2020 with stricter targets for CO_2 emission reductions. But it should be noted that rearmament and the economic crisis subsequently relativised all these advances. Overall, it is doubtful whether the EU's efforts will be sufficient in view of the impending global climate catastrophe, while this course also reflects a relativisation of the liberal free-market line.

On other issues, too, the EU's line on regulation has shifted towards security. Data protection and privacy is perhaps the most obvious example, where the 'Brussels effect' today tends to prioritise factors such as self-determination, sovereignty, and protection over the logic of absolute prosperity gains. Because of the size and influence of the European Single Market, the repercussions are felt by manufacturers from Silicon Valley to São Paulo, Seoul, and Shenzhen. Since the late 2000s the EU has also asserted its regulatory role more strategically in its relations with third states, further underlining its global reach. But the public debate has failed to keep up with the changes and interest in these global processes is thin on the ground.

The Covid-19 pandemic also expedited the tendency to prioritise security. The initial response of the EU and its member states in early 2020 resembled the 'refugee crisis' of 2015. Faced with an emergency outside the scope of European rules and structures, national unilateralism prevailed: borders were closed haphazardly, initial medical and financial measures had a very national focus, and certain leading commentators feared it would be the end of the EU. Yet, despite the EU's extremely limited powers in the area of pandemic response and health more generally, the trajectory ultimately looks more similar to the euro crisis. Tried and tested mechanisms were employed, but with significant innovations extending well beyond the status quo. The EU created a digital Covid certificate to facilitate transnational travel and agreed on a vaccine strategy that included development, manufacturing, and deployment. While the Union clearly prioritised the health and safety of its own citizens, it also donated hundreds of millions of vaccine doses. Instead of disintegrating, the EU again stumbled through by ad hoc deepening.

This applies especially to the summit decisions of December 2020, which gave the green light to a gigantic economic recovery package, commonly known as Next Generation EU. A significant part of the unprecedented sum of €750 billion was raised through joint borrowing, also a first. The approach remained controversial. It would have been an absolute no-go during the euro crisis just a few years earlier and heralded a radical rupture with the austerity policy adopted at that time. As well as deepening the Economic and Monetary Union, it stood for a fundamental shift away from the course associated with ECB policies and the 'frugal' priorities of Germany, the Netherlands, and other member states a decade earlier. The fact that Angela Merkel – the same Merkel who had so strongly influenced the line taken during the euro crisis – supported this decision is an issue for future historians to fully explain. Certainly, fear of the immense costs of a fragmented Single Market if hard-hit countries were left without support played an important role. Governments in southern Europe in particular had long argued that the EU should be given the right to borrow money on the markets and redistribute it among member states, since the Union would be able to secure more favourable rates than some of its member states. In that sense, Next Generation EU had a long prehistory.

5.2 Closing and Bolting the Door

In general ideas often simmer for quite a while before they are realised in the EU. It remains to be seen whether Next Generation EU will be a one-off exception or the beginning of a new, debt-financed policy that will expand the Union's powers even further. The 2025 decision to fund the Ukraine with a loan of €90 billion points in the latter direction. What can certainly be said is that Next Generation EU strengthened the EU's technocratic bent: the key documents were co-authored by national and EU elites, whereas national parliaments and the European Parliament remained marginal, as did social movements, trade unions, and other civil society actors. Providing economic support did not necessarily mean involving those affected.

Just as important, but largely under the radar, was the ECB's dramatic expansion of the money supply, which also helped keep the member states' economies afloat (Figure 5.7). Both moves – collective borrowing and monetary expansion – involve major medium-term risks, and it remains unclear what effect they will have on public confidence in the EU. There can be no doubt, however, that the integration process has just witnessed another very rapid and significant deepening. Yet again the modus operandi was largely to draw on long-established (or at least long-discussed) economic instruments, but to turn them to new purposes.

The new emphasis on protection is also apparent in other areas. Beyond EU-wide approval and procurement of Covid vaccines, increasing discussion about strategic autonomy and 'friendshoring' supply chains suggests a turn away from the 'open markets' logic of the 1990s and 2000s. Thus, the idea of autonomy is applied to a growing number of additional questions.

5 Security First: Course Correction, since 2009

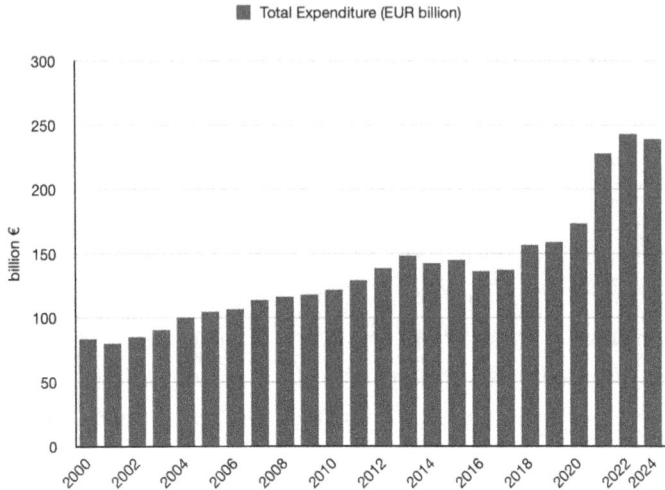

FIGURE 5.7 Evolution of the EU budget, 2000–2024. The substantial increase is just as remarkable as the absence of any significant drop after Brexit – despite the fact that for many years the United Kingdom had been the third largest contributor.

At the same time the pandemic is a bellwether for the increasing pressure on supranational forms of cooperation and especially of multilateralism, be it the UN framework or global trade. Transatlantic cooperation of the kind that saved the European banking system in 2015 – through secret talks between the US Federal Reserve and the ECB – is unthinkable under Donald J. Trump. The global ascendency of the autonomy paradigm squeezes the scope for multilateral cooperation and the EU's universalist bent – except where external pressures dictate otherwise. In that sense, Putin's war against Ukraine has helped to mend intra-European tensions and rifts – or at least to obscure them temporarily. At the same time a very broadly couched concept of security has supplanted the predominance of the economic.

Questions

1. Trace the causes of the change from the EU's form of liberalisation to a focus on security. Give an example.
2. Why was it technically so difficult for the United Kingdom to implement Brexit?
3. Explain the idea of the EU 'failing forward' on important issues during this period. Give an example. Is this a convincing interpretation?

Conclusion

The media tends to portray a European Union lurching from one crisis to the next. And in this brief history I have had plenty to say about problems, dangers, risks, and threats in the decades-long process of European integration. The founders were well aware of this aspect. Jean Monnet always believed that 'Europe would be built through crisis, and that it would be the sum of their solutions'.[1] Indeed, the European Union – as the European Communities before it – does seem to have a knack for turning crises to its advantage. Rather than leading to any kind of reversal, challenges have tended to reorient and expand the European project. So, we should not get carried away by excitable headlines, which often fail to do justice to the EU's complex and sometimes contradictory trajectory.

There was no master plan for incremental expansion and transformation, nor for a value-driven project. Nor was today's European Union simply created by the Brussels bureaucracy. Integration occurred because complicated negotiating and learning processes led the member states and other actors in that direction. Since the very beginning, the European project has been an engine

---

[1] Jean Monnet, *Memoirs* (Garden City, NY: Doubleday, 1979), p. 417.

of compromise and facilitation. While the goal of an 'ever closer union' has been in the treaties since the 1950s, it has come about more by accident than design.

That tendency was especially stark in the 1970s and has become so again since the 2010s. Amidst endless talk about problems and weaknesses, the integration process has progressed by leaps and bounds – adding new powers and new members, and opening up accession perspectives where none had been imaginable. Interestingly these steps occurred in areas outside the foundational treaties and sometimes began in the form of informal collaborations and minor initiatives that are only identifiable as milestones in retrospect.

Today's EU has experienced three transformative periods. The communities created in the 1950s focused on economic issues as the key to further integration. Although the EC's impact initially remained limited, its supranational elements set it apart from other international organisations. The second transformation began with informal processes in the 1970s. By the 1980s the EC was Europe's most prominent and influential organisation. While economics remained central, the EU had acquired many new dimensions by the 1990s and was exhibiting increasingly universalist aspirations, claiming moral authority within and far beyond its borders. The third transformation has been under way since the late 2000s, with a shift from various notions of freedom to security as the prime concern. In many ways, the EU fails to live up to the expectations associated with it. The reform processes remain generally reactive and incremental, the reconfigurations largely informal. Most ordinary people are blithely unaware of the growing power

Conclusion

and new priorities of the European project – or of its increasing fragility.

The significance European integration has acquired over the past decades is ultimately the principal reason for writing this book. If the EU had remained as marginal as it was in its early days (or as peripheral as its erstwhile institutional rivals) it would hardly have merited our attention. In other words, it is the topic's contemporary status that lends it its historical significance. The history shows us above all how *improbable* it was that the EU would achieve its current position.

Today the starting point of it all, the Europe of the 1950s, is a very distant and unfamiliar world. The long shadows that so coloured the early years – the Second World War, the Cold War, late colonialism, huge American influence in all spheres, including security, and rapidly increasing prosperity after deep economic turmoil and crisis – have little real effect today, even if they are still much discussed. Contextual factors since the 1970s and institutional transformations since the 1980s are much more important for the history of today's EU and the broader world: the fall of the Iron Curtain, globalisation and its limits, hopes of peace in Europe and their disappointment, and ecological disaster. The new social divisions and democratic challenges are more threatening than during the early days of the Cold War, while the world has become less ordered and predictable. On top of this, new global players like China and the return of the Russian threat create a new situation that may seem like a caricature of the Cold War, but in many respects follows a different logic. It is in this dramatically different Europe that the EU has become an increasingly central factor.

Conclusion

In all these phases, growing importance almost automatically meant new problems, for three reasons. First of all, integration has always triggered countervailing tendencies. Brexit is only the most obvious example. Norway's last-minute decision to withdraw its application in the 1970s showed that the Community was not necessarily predestined for unrelenting expansion. But loss of the United Kingdom has certainly not deterred the remaining member states from deepening their cooperation – and there are signs that the United Kingdom is cautiously edging towards a rapprochement. The shift of powers is another example: in some cases, they have moved from strictly national on to intergovernmental and finally to supranational. In other cases, however, we observe reverse processes, for instance with regard to the EU's powers to conclude international trade agreements. All in all, European integration is a highly dynamic process and not a matter of clear-cut permanent solutions.

Secondly, it was generally impossible to find comprehensive overall solutions; complex negotiations involving many parties tended to end at the lowest common denominator. In this way one integration step tended to lead to another, in order to plug gaps and deal with ensuing problems. For example, although successive treaty reforms were mooted during the two-and-a-bit decades between the Single European Act and the Treaty of Lisbon, there was no 'grand solution'. Or, to cite another example, the euro crisis demanded a whole set of additional measures to address the common currency's original defects. In most cases the decision makers and the informed public had always been aware of the deficits. Similar constellations are found much earlier, too. Even

Conclusion

FIGURE C.1 Ukrainian President Volodymyr Zelenskyy and European Commission President Ursula von der Leyen during a press conference on 4 November 2023. Credit: Getty Images: 1774804762.

when negotiations involved just six governments, they rarely achieved truly satisfactory outcomes. Today it is infinitely more difficult, with centrifugal forces so much stronger at all levels and the process itself under so much closer scrutiny in the member states and the wider world. The EU's decision of December 2023 to open accession talks with Ukraine illustrates both aspects (Figure C.1). It highlights the EU's enhanced attraction and importance in light of the Russian threat – but also presents enormous challenges: self-evidently in the security sphere but also for example in relation to the Common Agricultural Policy.

Thirdly, the growing pressures raised tricky questions around legitimisation of innovations. Law has always played a key role in European integration, and there has never been any shortage of formal decisions, directives, and regulations. But it has been considerably more difficult to generate public acceptance or to integrate viable participatory and transparency mechanisms into the institutional set-up. That challenge is much greater today because the contemporary EU's influence over the societies of its member states (and beyond) is so much stronger than in earlier decades. While checks and balances are desirable, they impair the organisation's ability to act quickly and flexibly. The same can be said of participation. This problem is found in every political order and is not specific to the EU. But it is especially pressing in the European project, and exacerbated by the trend towards differentiated integration, where member states may abstain from specific initiatives.

The constant pressure that characterises the integration process also points to a paradox. The extent to which the EU emerged and developed through real or perceived crises has made it astonishingly resilient and robust. The reasons for this are substantive, organisational, procedural, and political. Substantively many crises were not just challenges to European integration; they also affected other forms of government and administration, be they nation states or other international forums such as the United Nations and the Council of Europe. So, solutions were often discussed simultaneously at multiple levels. National unilateralism frequently fell short, as did the options of civil society engagement or alternative international mechanisms. The specific approach of European integration – an exceptionally close form of cooperation between states, an unusually strong legal framework, and an economic logic backed by substantial financial resources of its own – astonishingly often

Conclusion

turned out to be the most viable approach. To paraphrase Winston Churchill's quip: Brussels will always do the right thing – but only after first trying out all the alternatives. As already noted, the parties involved in the integration process often took only half a step forward (or one step forward and half a step to the side) so that new solutions always generated new problems of their own.

The Matthew effect – 'to those that have shall be given' – ensured that initial organisational advantages snowballed over time. After more than seven decades, the *acquis communautaire* and the institutional configuration contain layer upon layer of interests and compromises. The stock of prior decisions – and the interests and values they entail – form an immensely strong bond and exert a certain centripetal effect. If one side falls short in today's compromise, they will try to make it up in tomorrow's proposal. The size of the EU's budget makes it especially attractive to potential beneficiaries, be they individual member states, economic sectors such as agriculture, or civil society groups. The same applies to the immensely profitable internal market. Although accounting for overall costs and benefits is a great deal more difficult than quantifying concrete budget payments from Brussels, the common market remains the glue that holds the Union together. More broadly, unpicking all or parts of these complex arrangements would be associated with enormous risks. Nothing demonstrated that more clearly than the United Kingdom's extremely complicated and protracted departure from the Union following the Brexit referendum of 2016. However the future relationship between the EU and its insular neighbour turns out, one thing is certain: a quick, clean break is not possible. The reality still looks more like a festering wound. That said, the problems are significantly greater on the British side than the EU's. As various governments have said over the years, if the EU were to vanish, it would have to be reconstituted – in part at least – the very next day. All that underlines the organisational resilience of the integration process.

The EU is also extremely robust procedurally, enjoying a very secure legal foundation but malleable enough to adapt to continuously changing circumstances. In certain matters the legal framework itself fostered dynamic new developments, with the European Court of Justice often leading the charge. The European Commission and European Parliament also represent institutional voices often pressing for deepening. During her first term as Commission President (2019–2024), Ursula von der Leyen proposed a European Green Deal to tackle climate change; since 2022 the Russian invasion of Ukraine has been centre stage. The gigantic economic recovery programme launched to address the consequences of the Covid-19 pandemic – Next Generation EU – offers a further example of a long-discussed approach instituted rapidly in a moment of crisis. Here, despite its institutional deficits, the EU was able to translate a global crisis into a drastic increase in importance. This was, namely, the Union's first venture into collective borrowing – a truly revolutionary step, coming on the heels of expanded powers in the sphere of health. Two factors are often central to such leaps in integration. Firstly, ideas for reforms have often been on the table for a long time, waiting for their time to come. In view of the many players involved, almost every possibility has already been thought up, written down, and discussed somewhere. Secondly, the different political levels within the European Union have become immensely closely connected, especially since the 1980s. Peacefully and legalistically, European integration has steadily nudged the nation states in a post-classical direction and interwoven them at different levels like no other process.

Politically, finally, global and national processes have mitigated towards European integration. 'Project Europe' was closely associated with the idea of peace, especially in societies that experienced dictatorship and/or occupation during the bloody twentieth century. There was much talk of a 'community of values' and, above all in the period from the 1990s to the late 2000s, the EU came to be seen (and saw itself) as the standard-bearer of universalist ideals such as rule of law, democracy, and multilateralism. That applied particularly strongly to those parts of the continent that had experienced dictatorship and occupation – and explains why the United Kingdom and Switzerland were less enthusiastic. In countries that had suffered under authoritarianism, even minor technical decisions could be justified as a contribution to a better, peaceful future. Among the decision-making elites there was also a broad consensus that unpopular reforms at the national level would only be accepted if they could be presented as external necessities. The Italians call this *vincolo esterno*, and the idea plays an important role throughout the Union. As a welcome side effect, national politicians were able to claim credit for successes while scapegoating Brussels wherever difficulties arose.

At the same time, global political tensions and threats created powerful incentives for closer cooperation. Like collective hopes, shared fear drew different sides together and paved the ground for reciprocal concessions. Exogenous pressure was a recurring factor bringing the member states together. We will never know whether the first precursors of today's EU would have come into being without the anti-communist motivation and the system confrontation of the Cold War. The same applies to the Treaties of Rome and the Suez crisis that underlined the decline of European colonial power. More recently, it took the invasion of Ukraine in 2022 for the western part of the continent to acknowledge the threat from Putin's Russia. That coming together has boosted the focus on security that had been emerging since the late 2000s and has granted the EU new attractiveness and additional powers.

The shift in focus from economics to security represents a major change for the EU. The glass is half full and half empty: compared to the past, the EU has gained many new powers. However, in view of the challenges, these continue to be insufficient. The EU resembles a professional soccer player who suddenly finds himself on a rugby field. It remains to be seen whether the Union can cope with this strange (and much more brutal) new world.

Further integration is by no means a foregone conclusion. The more important the EU has become, the greater the controversy. Criticism of the kind of supranational cooperation for which the united Europe stands has grown immensely, especially over the past two decades; illiberalism and nationalism are but the two most prominent keywords in this connection. At the same time the great crises of our age are leading to a serious rethinking of priorities and alternatives. As well as scepticism and criticism, such debates brought to light a great deal of support for the EU. At a more fundamental level, debate is an indispensable aspect of democratic politics. Given the EU's importance, nothing would be less appropriate than silent harmony. Instead, debate needs to be better channelled and directed towards finding solutions. There is no denying that certain issues have been dealt with too hastily and with inadequate discussion; one example would be the unprecedented Covid recovery package, which may yet come back to bite the integration project.

Integration is not a one-way process either. The edge cases of Algeria and Greenland notwithstanding, it was Brexit that highlighted the reversibility of European integration. As the stakes have grown, so too has the number of existential challenges. And the greater the EU's ambition to address central global political issues – such as the climate crisis, global migration, international conflicts, and a fragile financial capitalism system – by promoting its own shared values, the greater the risk of failure and disappointment. That applies especially in relation to past and future support for Ukraine, where popular enthusiasm in the member states is increasingly tenuous.

Many citizens in the member states are not exactly euphoric about the EU. This closes certain possibilities but opens up others. Instead of abstract debates about topics like the ultimate destination of the integration process, pragmatism is the order of the day; practical rather than utopian, with courage and patience, moral direction, and flexibility. That also means dispensing with hollow phrases and outdated ideas and acknowledging that the EU has become an innovative hybrid between national statehood and European federalism:

a *demoi-cracy*, as Kalypso Nicolaïdis described it, in which national and EU citizenship are melded and where the central principles of governance – in particular rule of law and the welfare state – are still handled primarily in the national framework.[2]

Today the EU seems to be 'too big to fail'. It is also more susceptible to existential crisis than it ever has been. Time and again it has survived challenges. Very often, it has also turned them to its advantage – where they have appeared successively or it has been possible to divide parallel phenomena into separate issues. But if multiple challenges appear simultaneously and in negative symbiosis, existential crisis looms: for example, if moves by one or more members to leave were to become bound up with economic turmoil, erosion of Community law, and military conflicts. Another euro crisis could quickly become existential, especially if the problems emanated from a large member state like France or Italy. Despite efforts since the late 2000s to secure the common currency, the euro's flaws could yet bring down the entire edifice. Failing forward, as the prevalent problem-solving mode since the late 2000s, should not be mistaken for a truly sustainable and robust solution. But even in the event of collapse, a core of states would likely create something similar; too high the price of not cooperating. Quite generally, defunct international organisations tend to have vigorous afterlives.

The greater danger is illiberal transformation from within. The complexity of Brexit has given pause to

---

[2] Kalypso Nicolaïdis, 'Our European Demoi-cracy: Is this Constitution a Third Way for Europe?', in Kalypso Nicolaïdis and Stephen Weatherill (eds.), *Whose Europe? National Models and the Constitution of the European Union* (Oxford: Oxford University Press, 2003), pp. 137–152.

many illiberal groups, especially those on the far-right margins. Rather than leaving, their strategy is now to attack the already weak system of values and erode forms of solidarity among member states. Instead, they seek to return many powers to the national level – although they are still more than happy to profit from 'Europe' where they can, for example by way of subsidies. Moves in this direction are increasingly showing effects. The EU is especially ill-prepared for this challenge – which is particularly dangerous because it comes in incremental stealth.

So, the status quo offers no grounds for complacency. Some would argue that the EU has been gripped by megalomania and is now paying the price. I would suggest that reports of its imminent demise are greatly exaggerated. Others would say that the EU has finally got down to *realpolitik*: tackling the really big, relevant problems while improvising to arrive at genuinely political decisions rather than seeking laborious consensus within a tight corset of rules. In fact, the EU is much more similar to other 'normal' political actors than it ever wanted to admit. It would do well to see itself as such and communicate accordingly.

A new beginning is certainly needed, for reasons internal and external. Whether we are looking at war, climate, migration, social affairs, economic issues, or values, an increasingly complex and dangerous world demands collective solutions. For many decades Project Europe was able to go about its business undisturbed, shielded behind other institutions and frameworks. Today, in its third period of massive transformation, it has certainly grown out of that cocoon. The EU has increasingly become a

Conclusion

project of security. Over the past decade the world has become much more dangerous and much less predictable. Under Trump, the United States has become one of Europe's harshest critics. The EU will have to acknowledge that the global rules are changing dramatically, and becoming much more brutal. In order to secure its achievements and attain new, ambitious goals it will have to become a truly proactive force both internally and externally.

Questions

1. What are the most likely scenarios in which the EU could fall into existential crisis? Why?
2. What role has external pressure – from other states and regions – played in the integration process?
3. What are the historical connections between crises and the process of European integration?

CHRONOLOGY

1940s

4–11 February 1945	Yalta Conference on the reorganisation of post-war Germany and Europe
17 July–12 August 1945	Potsdam Conference on the post-war order
19 September 1946	Winston Churchill's speech at the University of Zurich on creating a united Europe
28 March 1947	United Nations Economic Commission for Europe (UNECE) is established
5 June 1947	George C. Marshall gives a speech launching the Marshall Plan
30 October 1947	General Agreement on Tariffs and Trade (GATT) is created
17 March 1948	Brussels Treaty is signed
16 April 1948	Organisation for European Economic Co-operation (OEEC) is established
7–11 May 1948	Congress of Europe in The Hague
4 April 1949	North Atlantic Treaty Organization (NATO) is created
5 May 1949	Council of Europe is established

1950s

9 May 1950	Schuman Declaration

Chronology

24 October 1950	French Prime Minister René Pleven presents his plan to create a European army
4 November 1950	The member states of the Council of Europe sign the European Convention on Human Rights in Rome
18 April 1951	Paris Treaty, establishing the European Coal and Steel Community (ECSC)
27 May 1952	The six ECSC member states sign a treaty to create the European Defence Community (EDC)
23 July 1952	ECSC Treaty enters into force
10 March 1953	Draft treaty creating a European Political Community
30 August 1954	French parliament vetoes the EDC Treaty, thus also aborting the planned European Political Community
23 October 1954	Building on the Brussels Pact Organisation, the Western European Union (WEU) is established
6 May 1955	The Federal Republic of Germany joins NATO
1–2 June 1955	The foreign ministers of the ECSC states meet for a conference in Messina
13 October 1955	Jean Monnet establishes the Action Committee for the United States of Europe
29 May 1956	Venice Conference: the foreign ministers of the ECSC states declare their intention to establish a common market and a nuclear energy organisation
October–November 1956	Suez crisis

Chronology

25 March 1957	The Treaties of Rome are signed, creating the European Economic Community (EEC) and the European Atomic Energy Community (Euratom)
7 January 1958	The EEC starts its work, with German Walter Hallstein as the first Commission President

1960s

4 January 1960	European Free Trade Association (EFTA) is established
1 October 1960	The OEEC becomes the Organisation for Economic Co-operation and Development (OECD) and accepts Canada and the United States as new members
9 July 1961	Association agreement between the EEC and Greece
July–August 1961	Denmark, Ireland, and the United Kingdom submit official applications to join the EEC
2 November 1961	The French government presents a proposal for a 'Union of States' (Fouchet I)
14 January 1962	First important agreements on the nascent Common Agricultural Policy (CAP)
18 January 1962	Second draft of the Fouchet plan (Fouchet II)
17 April 1962	Negotiations on the Fouchet plans fail
30 April 1962	Norway submits its official application to join the EEC
1 July 1962	After a referendum on independence from France, Algeria is no longer part of the EEC

Chronology

14 January 1963	French President Charles de Gaulle vetoes the United Kingdom's EEC accession, also halting the accession process of the other candidates
22 January 1963	Élysée Treaty of Friendship between France and West Germany
5 February 1963	Van Gend en Loos judgement of the European Court of Justice (ECJ)
20 July 1963	The EEC and eighteen African states sign an association agreement in Yaoundé (Cameroon)
12 September 1963	Association agreement between the EEC and Turkey
15 July 1964	Costa/ENEL judgement of the ECJ
8 April 1965	Treaty merging the executives of the ECSC, the EEC, and Euratom to establish the European Community (EC)
1 June 1965	The crisis of the empty chair begins
28–30 January 1966	Luxembourg Compromise
10–11 May 1967	Second application by the British, Irish, and Danish governments to join the EEC
6 July 1967	Jean Rey (Belgium) is appointed President of the EC Commission, the second person to hold this office after Hallstein
21 July 1967	Norway again applies for EC membership
27 November 1967	For a second time, French President Charles de Gaulle vetoes EC membership for the United Kingdom
1 July 1968	Beginning of the EEC's customs union, eighteen months earlier than planned
29 July 1969	Yaoundé II is signed

Chronology

1–2 December 1969	Summit meeting in The Hague lays the basis for important steps during the 1970s, including the EC's first enlargement

1970s

21 April 1970	Council decision to grant the EC its own resources
2 July 1970	Franco Maria Malfatti (Italy) becomes the third President of the EC Commission
8 October 1970	Werner plan for the creation of an economic and monetary union
27 October 1970	Davignon report proposes cooperation on foreign policy; starting point of the European Political Cooperation (EPC)
15 August 1971	US government unilaterally ends the direct convertibility of the dollar to gold; 'Nixon shock'
22 January 1972	Denmark, Ireland, Norway, and the United Kingdom sign their accession treaties. Norway withdraws from the process after a referendum on 25 September
22 March 1972	After Malfatti's resignation, Sicco Mansholt (Netherlands) becomes the fourth President of the EC Commission
24 April 1972	'Currency snake' created to coordinate the monetary policy of the EC member states
19–21 October 1972	Paris summit: important decisions in several EC policy fields
1 January 1973	Denmark, Ireland, and the United Kingdom join the EC, increasing the number of member states to nine

Chronology

6 January 1973	François-Xavier Ortoli (France) becomes the fifth President of the EC Commission
3 July 1973	Conference on Security and Cooperation in Europe opens in Helsinki
1 April 1974	British government requests renegotiation of its accession treaty
9–10 December 1974	Paris summit: the European Council becomes a permanent institution
28 February 1975	Lomé Convention with states in the Global South succeeds the Yaoundé Convention
5 June 1975	Referendum in the United Kingdom: 67 per cent vote to remain in the EC
12 June 1975	Greece submits its official application to join the EEC
29 December 1975	Tindemans report on 'European integration'
20 September 1976	Decision to hold direct elections to the European Parliament
6 January 1977	Roy Jenkins (UK) becomes the sixth President of the EC Commission
28 March 1977	Portugal submits its official application to join the EEC
28 July 1977	Spain submits its official application to join the EEC
4–5 December 1978	European Council in Brussels agrees on the introduction of the European Monetary System
20 February 1979	Cassis de Dijon judgement of the ECJ
13 March 1979	European Monetary System comes into effect

Chronology

7–10 June 1979	First direct elections to the European Parliament
31 October 1979	Lomé II Convention

1980s

1 January 1981	Greece becomes the EC's tenth member state
6 January 1981	Gaston Thorn (Luxembourg) becomes the seventh President of the EC Commission
19 November 1981	Foreign ministers Emilio Colombo (Italy) and Hans-Dietrich Genscher (West Germany) present their plan on reforming the EC
23 February 1982	Referendum on EC membership in Greenland (then a part of Denmark): 53 per cent vote to leave
25 January 1983	Agreement on a Common Fisheries Policy
17–19 June 1983	European Council meeting in Stuttgart adopts the 'Solemn Declaration on European Union'
14 February 1984	European Parliament adopts the Draft Treaty Establishing the European Union
14–17 June 1984	Second direct elections to the European Parliament
25–26 June 1984	European Council meeting at Fontainebleau: British budget question solved; creation of the Dooge Committee on institutional reform and the Adonnino Committee on a people's Europe
8 December 1984	Lomé III Convention
6 January 1985	Jacques Delors (France) becomes the eighth President of the European Commission

Chronology

1 February 1985	Greenland leaves the EC and becomes an associated member
12 June 1985	Portugal and Spain sign their accession treaties and become member states the following January
14 June 1985	The European Commission publishes a White Book on completing the internal market
14 June 1985	The first Schengen Agreement is signed
28–29 June 1985	European Council meeting in Milan agrees on an intergovernmental conference to revise the Treaties of Rome
17 and 28 February 1986	The EC member states sign the Single European Act (SEA)
29 May 1986	The European flag is raised in Brussels for the first time, to the strains of the 'Ode to Joy'
11–13 February 1987	European Council meeting in Brussels approves the Delors I package, with reforms to the EC's own resources and structural funds
14 April 1987	Turkey submits its official application to join the EEC
15 June 1987	European Council meeting agrees on the Erasmus programme
1 July 1987	SEA enters into force
25 June 1988	Declaration on the establishment of official relations between the EC and Comecon
27–28 June 1988	European Council meeting in Hannover renews Delors's presidency of the European Commission and decides to set up a committee to move towards an Economic and Monetary Union (EMU)

Chronology

20 September 1988	Margaret Thatcher's Bruges speech warning against a 'European superstate'
12 April 1989	Delors's report on an Economic and Monetary Union
15–18 June 1989	Third direct elections to the European Parliament
17 July 1989	Austria submits its official application to join the EEC
19 September 1989	EC signs an economic agreement with Poland
9 November 1989	The Berlin Wall falls
8–9 December 1989	European Council meeting in Strasbourg decides to convene an intergovernmental conference on the EMU and adopts the Community Charter of Fundamental Social Rights for Workers
15 December 1989	Lomé IV Convention

1990s

28 April 1990	Special European Council meeting in Dublin defines a common approach to German unification and relations with states of east-central and eastern Europe
15 June 1990	Twelve EC member states agree on the Dublin Convention on responsibility for examining asylum applications
19 June 1990	Schengen Convention supplementing the Schengen Agreement
25–26 June 1990	European Council meeting in Dublin sets dates for intergovernmental conferences on the EMU and political union

Chronology

1 July 1990	First stage of the EMU begins
4 July 1990	Cyprus submits its official application to join the EEC
16 July 1990	Malta submits its official application to join the EEC
3 October 1990	German unification; the former East Germany becomes part of the EEC
14–15 December 1990	European Council meeting in Rome: intergovernmental conferences on the EMU and political union begin
21 May 1991	Agreement to reform the Common Agricultural Policy
25 June 1991	Slovenia and Croatia declare their independence; start of fighting and wars in (former) Yugoslavia
1 July 1991	Sweden submits its official application to join the EEC
1 July 1991	Warsaw Pact is dissolved
22 October 1991	EC and EFTA states decide to form the European Economic Area (EEA) as of 1993
9–10 December 1991	European Council meeting in Maastricht agrees on a draft Treaty on European Union
16 December 1991	The EC signs 'European agreements' with Poland, Hungary, and Czechoslovakia
7 February 1992	Member states sign the Treaty on European Union in Maastricht (Treaty of Maastricht)
18 March 1992	Finland submits its official application to join the EU
20 May 1992	Switzerland submits its official application to join the EU
21 May 1992	The Council of Ministers agrees on a reform of the Common

Chronology

	Agricultural Policy (MacSharry reform)
2 June 1992	In a referendum, Denmark votes 50.7 per cent against ratification of the Treaty of Maastricht
20 September 1992	In a referendum, France approves the Treaty of Maastricht by a narrow majority of 51 per cent
25 November 1992	Norway submits its official application to join the EU
6 December 1992	In a referendum in Switzerland, 50.3 per cent reject accession to the European Economic Area
11–12 December 1992	European Council meeting in Edinburgh adopts opt-out clauses for Denmark and approves the Delors II package on structural and financial measures
1 January 1993	European Single Market enters into force
18 May 1993	In a second referendum, Denmark agrees to the Treaty of Maastricht with a majority of 56.7 per cent
21–22 June 1993	At a meeting in Copenhagen, the European Council lays down the economic and political criteria for EU accession of candidate countries (Copenhagen Criteria)
1 November 1993	Treaty of Maastricht enters into force
15 December 1993	GATT Uruguay Round ends with an important decision to liberalise trade and agreement to create the World Trade Organization (WTO)
1 January 1994	The second stage of the EMU begins
1 January 1994	European Economic Area comes into effect

Chronology

31 March 1994	Hungary submits its official application to join the EU
5 April 1994	Poland submits its official application to join the EU
9–12 June 1994	Fourth direct elections to the European Parliament
28 November 1994	A referendum in Norway rejects membership
1 January 1995	Austria, Finland, and Sweden become member states
23 January 1995	Jacques Santer (Luxembourg) becomes the ninth President of the EU Commission
26 March 1995	Schengen Agreement enters into force with initially seven member states
22 June 1995	Romania submits its official application to join the EU
27 June 1995	Slovakia submits its official application to join the EU
26 July 1995	Signing of the EUROPOL Convention
27 October 1995	Latvia submits its official application to join the EU
4 November 1995	Revision of the Lomé IV Convention
28 November 1995	Estonia submits its official application to join the EU
8 December 1995	Lithuania submits its official application to join the EU
15 December 1995	Framework agreement on cooperation with MERCOSUR
15–16 December 1995	European Council meeting in Madrid sets date of 1 January 1999 for introduction of the euro

Chronology

16 December 1995	Bulgaria submits its official application to join the EU
17 January 1996	Czech Republic submits its official application to join the EU
29 March 1996	Intergovernmental conference to revise the Treaty of Maastricht begins
10 June 1996	Slovenia submits its official application to join the EU
16–17 June 1997	European Council meeting in Amsterdam establishes the political basis for the Stability and Growth Pact
1 September 1997	Dublin Convention of 1990 enters into force
2 October 1997	Signing of the Treaty of Amsterdam
12–13 December 1997	European Council meeting in Luxembourg: decision to launch a comprehensive enlargement process
31 March 1998	Start of official accession negotiations with Estonia, Poland, Slovenia, the Czech Republic, Hungary, and Cyprus
3 May 1998	Heads of state and government determine that eleven EU states meet the criteria for adopting the euro
1 June 1998	European Central Bank opens in Frankfurt am Main
31 December 1998	Meeting of the economics and finance ministers of the eleven euro countries fixes the euro conversion rates for the participating currencies
1 January 1999	EMU's third stage begins: introduction of the euro as book money
15 March 1999	EU Commission resigns following the publication of a report on fraud, mismanagement, and nepotism

Chronology

1 May 1999	Treaty of Amsterdam enters into force
3–4 June 1999	European Council meeting in Cologne: Javier Solana (Spain) becomes the High Representative of the Union for Foreign Affairs and Security Policy
10–13 June 1999	Fifth direct elections to the European Parliament
18 September 1999	Romano Prodi (Italy) becomes the tenth President of the European Commission
15–16 October 1999	European Council meeting in Tampere, the first at which Justice and Home Affairs is the focal point
10–11 December 1999	European Council meeting in Helsinki agrees on an intergovernmental conference on treaty revision and decides to start accession negotiations with twelve governments

2000s

14 February 2000	Intergovernmental conference on institutional reform of the EU begins
15 February 2000	Accession negotiations begin with Bulgaria, Latvia, Lithuania, Malta, Romania, and Slovakia
23–24 March 2000	Special European Council adopts the Lisbon strategy
23 June 2000	Cotonou Agreement replaces Lomé IV Convention
28 September 2000	Denmark votes against introducing the euro
7–10 December 2000	European Council agrees on the Treaty of Nice and proclaims the

Chronology

	European Charter of Fundamental Rights
1 January 2001	Greece becomes the twelfth member of the Eurozone
26 February 2001	Signing of the Treaty of Nice
7 June 2001	Referendum in Ireland rejects the Treaty of Nice with 53.9 per cent
11 September 2001	Terror attacks in the United States
14–15 December 2001	European Council in Laken establishes a convention on the institutional and political future of the EU
1 January 2002	Introduction of the euro as cash in twelve EU member states
28 February 2002	European Convention ('Constitutional Convention') begins its work
23 July 2002	ECSC treaty ends
19 October 2002	Ireland holds a second referendum on the Treaty of Nice; 63 per cent vote in favour
12–13 December 2002	European Council agrees in Copenhagen on the accession of Cyprus, the Czech Republic, Estonia, Hungary, Latvia, Lithuania, Malta, Poland, Slovakia, and Slovenia by 2004
1 February 2003	Treaty of Nice enters into force
18 February 2003	European Council agrees on Dublin II Regulation on asylum law
21 February 2003	Croatia submits its official application to join the EU
16 April 2003	Accession treaties for ten future member states signed in Athens
19–20 June 2003	Thessaloniki European Council: president of the Constitutional

	Convention presents the draft Treaty establishing a Constitution for Europe (TCE)
4 October 2003	Start of the intergovernmental conference on the TCE
13 January 2004	European Commission proposes a regulation on services in the internal market
22 March 2004	Macedonia submits its official application to join the EU
1 May 2004	Cyprus, the Czech Republic, Estonia, Hungary, Latvia, Lithuania, Malta, Poland, Slovakia, and Slovenia join the EU, which now has twenty-five member states
10–13 June 2004	Sixth direct elections to the European Parliament
17–18 June 2004	European Council meeting in Brussels: agreement on the TCE
26 October 2004	European Border and Coast Guard Agency (FRONTEX) is set up to support management of the EU's external borders
29 October 2004	EU member states sign the TCE in Rome
22 November 2004	José Manuel Barroso (Portugal) becomes the eleventh President of the EU Commission
25 April 2005	Bulgaria and Romania sign their accession treaties in Luxembourg
29 May 2005	TCE: 55.7 per cent vote no in France
1 June 2005	TCE: 61.6 per cent vote no in the Netherlands
16–17 June 2005	European Council in Brussels agrees on a 'pause for reflection' on the TCE

Chronology

3 October 2005	Start of accession negotiations with Croatia and Turkey
29 May 2006	European Council agrees on a services directive for the internal market (Bolkestein Directive)
1 January 2007	Bulgaria and Romania join the EU, which now has twenty-seven member states
1 January 2007	Introduction of the euro in Slovenia
9 August 2007	Start of the international banking and financial crisis (subprime crisis)
13 December 2007	Signing of the Treaty of Lisbon
1 January 2008	Introduction of the euro in Malta and Cyprus as the fourteenth and fifteenth countries in the Eurozone
12 June 2008	Referendum in Ireland rejects the Lisbon Treaty by 53.4 per cent
1 September 2008	Summit meeting of EU heads of state and government to discuss the war in Georgia criticises Russia's 'disproportionate reaction'
11–12 December 2008	In addition to measures to reduce CO_2 emissions, the European Council adopts an economic stimulus programme of around €200 billion to counter the economic crisis
15 December 2008	Montenegro submits its official application to join the EU
1 January 2009	Slovakia is the sixteenth state to adopt the euro
28 April 2009	Albania submits its official application to join the EU
4–7 June 2009	Seventh direct elections to the European Parliament

Chronology

23 July 2009	Iceland submits its official application to join the EU
3 October 2009	Ireland adopts the Treaty of Lisbon in a second referendum
20 November 2009	Herman Van Rompuy (Belgium) becomes the first permanent President of the European Council; Catherine Ashton (UK) becomes High Representative of the EU for Foreign Affairs and Security Policy
1 December 2009	Treaty of Lisbon enters into force
22 December 2009	Serbia submits its official application to join the EU

2010s

2 May 2010	International Monetary Fund (IMF) and EU agree on an aid programme for Greece (a bailout of €110 billion)
11 May 2010	European Council adopts the European Financial Stabilisation Mechanism to protect the euro
7 June 2010	Creation of the European Financial Stability Facility to protect the euro
28 November 2010	EU and IMF agree on an €85 billion bailout for Ireland
1 January 2011	Estonia is the seventeenth country to adopt the euro
18 January 2011	Start of the first 'European Semester' to review national budget and reform proposals
16 May 2011	Agreement on a €78 billion EU and IMF bailout for Portugal
30 June 2011	Dissolution of the WEU
13 December 2011	Six legislative measures to reform the Stability and Growth Pact (the 'Six Pack')

Chronology

21 February 2012	Finance ministers approve second bailout for Greece (€130 billion)
2 March 2012	European Council: majority of EU states sign the European Fiscal Compact
9 June 2012	Spain receives financial aid from the EU, but avoids an official bailout
26 July 2012	European Central Bank President Mario Draghi declares that the ECB will do 'whatever it takes' to save the euro
27 September 2012	European Stability Mechanism enters into force
27 November 2012	Eurozone finance ministers and IMF reach agreement on second financial aid programme for Greece (bailout)
10 December 2012	EU receives the Nobel Peace Prize
25 March 2013	Cyprus receives financial aid from the EU and IMF (bailout)
30 May 2013	'Two pack' of EU regulations for stricter budget monitoring and economic governance
17 June 2013	EU and United States begin negotiations on a Transatlantic Trade and Investment Partnership (TTIP)
1 July 2013	Croatia joins the EU as the twenty-eighth member state
15 October 2013	European Council establishes the European Single Supervisory Mechanism as a step towards a banking union
21 November 2013	President Viktor Yanukovych unexpectedly decides not to sign Ukraine's association agreement with the EU, leading to nationwide protests and the Euromaidan

Chronology

15 December 2013	Ireland is the first member state to exit bailout
1 January 2014	Latvia is the eighteenth country to adopt the euro
1 January 2014	Dublin III Regulation enters into force
1 January 2014	End of last restrictions on the free movement of workers from Bulgaria and Romania
23 January 2014	Spain exits aid measures
5 March 2014	European Council adopts sanctions against Russia in response to the occupation of Crimea; many more to follow
17 May 2014	Portugal exits bailout
22–25 May 2014	Eighth direct elections to the European Parliament
15 July 2014	Establishment of the Single Resolution Mechanism as a step towards a banking union
30 July 2014	EU imposes new economic sanctions against Russia, following the downing of flight MH17 over eastern Ukraine
30 August 2014	European Council: Donald Tusk (Poland) becomes President of the European Council from 1 December; Federica Mogherini (Italy) becomes High Representative of the EU for Foreign Affairs and Security Policy as of 1 November
1 November 2014	Jean-Claude Juncker (Luxembourg) becomes the twelfth President of the EU Commission
1 January 2015	Lithuania is the nineteenth country to adopt the euro

Chronology

12 March 2015	Iceland withdraws its application for EU membership
14 July 2015	Agreement on a nuclear deal with Iran, negotiated with significant EU involvement
19 August 2015	Third bailout for Greece
20 August 2015	Macedonia declares state of emergency on its border with Greece
25 August 2015	Germany suspends Dublin procedures for refugees from Syria; from summer 2015, several member states reinstate border controls, challenging the Schengen system
12 November 2015	Summit on migration issues in Valletta with heads of state and government of African countries
12 December 2015	Paris Agreement on climate protection
15 February 2016	Bosnia and Herzegovina submits its official application to join the EU
20 February 2016	UK Prime Minister David Cameron announces a referendum on EU membership for 23 June
4 March 2016	European Commission proposes roadmap to return to the Schengen system
18 March 2016	Agreement between the EU and Turkey on asylum and refugees
31 March 2016	Cyprus exits bailout
23 June 2016	UK votes by 52 to 48 per cent to leave the EU: Prime Minister Cameron resigns the following day
30 October 2016	EU and Canada sign the CETA free trade agreement despite a 'no' vote by the Walloon regional parliament

Chronology

24 November 2016	European Parliament calls for suspension of accession negotiations with Turkey
1 March 2017	EU Commission presents the White Paper on the Future of Europe
29 March 2017	British Prime Minister Theresa May initiates the withdrawal procedure for the UK
1 September 2017	Association agreement with Ukraine enters into force
21 September 2017	CETA enters into force provisionally
11 December 2017	European Council decides to establish Permanent Structured Cooperation (PESCO) in the field of defence
12 December 2017	European Commission initiates rule of law proceedings against Poland
17 July 2018	EU and Japan conclude a free trade agreement
20 August 2018	Greece exits bailout
12 September 2018	European Parliament initiates rule of law proceedings against Hungary
25 November 2018	EU27 leaders endorse the draft Brexit withdrawal agreement
23–26 May 2019	Ninth direct elections to the European Parliament
17 October 2019	Renegotiated agreement between the UK and the EU
1 December 2019	Ursula von der Leyen (Germany) becomes the thirteenth President of the European Commission; Charles Michel (Belgium) becomes President of the European Council; Josep Borrell (Spain) becomes High Representative of the EU for Foreign Affairs and Security Policy

Chronology

10–11 December 2019	European Council decides that the EU should achieve climate neutrality by 2050

2020s

31 January 2020	United Kingdom withdraws from the EU on the basis of the agreement of 17 October 2019
12 March 2020	World Health Organization declares Covid-19 pandemic; many member states introduce temporary border controls and closures
21 December 2020	EU authorises the first Covid-19 vaccine
1 January 2021	EU–UK trade and cooperation agreement enters into force provisionally
12 February 2021	Formal establishment of the Next Generation EU recovery instrument worth €750 billion
22 March 2021	Council decision establishing the European Peace Facility
24 February 2022	Russian full-scale invasion of Ukraine; additional EU sanctions and other measures follow
28 February 2022	Ukraine submits its official application to join the EU
3 March 2022	Georgia and Moldovia submit their official applications to join the EU
1 January 2023	Croatia adopts the euro, becoming the twentieth country to join the Eurozone
14–15 December 2023	European Council decides to open accession negotiations with Ukraine

Chronology

	and Moldova; Georgia receives candidate country status
6–9 June 2024	Tenth direct elections to the European Parliament
1 December 2024	Ursula von der Leyen starts her second term as President of the European Commission
19 March 2025	European Commission publishes white paper on European defence, planning to spend €800 billion
3 April 2025	US President Donald Trump announces massive tariff increases, complex negotiations follow
19 May 2025	EU–UK deal on security, fisheries, and energy
27 June 2025	European Council adopts SAFE, a financial instrument for joint defence procurement
19 December 2025	EU greenlights a loan of €90 billion of funding for Ukraine
1 January 2026	Bulgaria adopts the euro, becoming the twenty-first member to join the Eurozone

BIBLIOGRAPHICAL ESSAY

B.1 Introduction

Every month the EU produces thousands of documents. And every month academics publish hundreds of papers dealing with the EU and its history in one way or another. So, this bibliography has to be highly selective. It begins with the most important primary sources. Many of these are easily accessible and provide a deeper understanding of the process that led to today's EU. The academic literature is listed by topic, concentrating on publications in English, but also including important works in other languages. Rather than proceeding chapter by chapter, the bibliography employs a combination of chronological and thematic categories.

Archival material is usually withheld for thirty years, so the historical research to date has concentrated on the Cold War period. For that era I am able to list many significant historiographical contributions, while there is also an older body of research from the social sciences (in particular political science and international relations, but also law, economics, and sociology). Because the thirty-year rule blocks archival sources, publications in the social sciences come to the fore in the discussion of more recent decades. The bibliography concentrates on key monographs and collections (only Section B.6 also contains articles: conceptual questions and historiography are often discussed in this format, rather than in books), from where it is comparably easy to find further literature, including texts published in journals.

Three English-language history journals are particularly important: *Contemporary European History*, the *European History Review* and the *Journal of European Integration History*. Journals are even more important in the social sciences, but the output is too vast and fast-moving to provide any meaningful overview. I therefore concentrate on listing handbooks and other comprehensive collections. While only presenting a tiny fraction of the available material, I hope the bibliography illustrates the richness of the debate and the plurality of approaches.

B.2 Primary Sources

There are many primary sources for this topic, in numerous languages. Quite a few of them are easily accessible for research and teaching. The EU institutions' own websites contain a wealth of historical documents, including treaties and directives, speeches and images.

EU institutions deposit their archival holdings at the Historical Archives of the European Union (HAEU) in Florence, where they are made available to the public under the thirty-year rule.[1] Many of these documents have been digitalised and are available online. The same is true of some of the HAEU's other collections, including private papers, documents on other international organisations such as the OECD, and interviews with key actors. The various EU institutions also have archives in Brussels, which hold additional documents. Especially for the period since the 1980s, it is also useful to consider their websites and holdings.

State archives are equally crucial for the history of European integration. Many of the national state archives have put their finding aids and documents at least partially online.

Two external collections stand out. The CVCE (www.cvce.eu) provides access to primary sources through multimedia collections in multiple languages, while the Archive of European Integration (https://aei.pitt.edu) has a more institutional orientation.

Many of the central figures involved in European integration published diaries, memoirs, and other texts. Some of these are

---

[1] www.eui.eu/en/academic-units/historical-archives-of-the-european-union

available in translation, others not. Some translations, such as the English version of the memoirs of Paul-Henri Spaak, are incomplete, so whenever possible, it is better to consult texts in their original language. There is a long list of biographies on top politicians such as Alcide de Gasperi, Robert Schuman, and Margaret Thatcher, many of which also discuss their role in European integration while not being exclusively dedicated to this matter. Newspapers, grey literature, and statistics can also be very helpful sources. Many of these are also available online (for Dutch newspapers, for instance, delpher.nl).

B.3 Pre-1945 Ideas of European Unity and Early Forms of Cooperation

Bussière, Éric, Michel Dumoulin and Sylvain Schirmann (eds.), *Europe organisée, Europe du libre-échange? Fin XIXe siècle–années 1960* (Brussels: Peter Lang, 2006).

D'Auria, Matthew and Jan Vermeiren (eds.), *Visions and Ideas of Europe during the First World War* (London: Routledge, 2019).

Ghervas, Stella, *Conquering Peace: From the Enlightenment to the European Union* (Cambridge, MA: Harvard University Press, 2021).

Gosewinkel, Dieter (ed.), *Anti-liberal Europe: A Neglected Story of Europeanization* (New York: Berghahn, 2015).

Hewitson, Mark and Matthew D'Auria (eds.), *Europe in Crisis: Intellectuals and the European Idea, 1917–1957* (New York: Berghahn, 2012).

Lipgens, Walter (ed.), *Documents on the History of European Integration*, 4 vols. (Berlin: De Gruyter, 1986–1991).

Pagden, Anthony, *The Pursuit of Europe: A History* (Oxford: Oxford University Press, 2022).

Pasture, Patrick, *Imagining European Unity since 1000 AD* (Basingstoke: Palgrave, 2015).

Schmale, Wolfgang, *Geschichte Europas* (Vienna: Böhlau, 2000).

Segers, Mathieu, *The Origins of European Integration: The Pre-History of Today's European Union, 1937–1951* (Cambridge: Cambridge University Press, 2023).

Spiering, Menno and Michael J. Wintle (eds.), *European Identity and the Second World War* (Basingstoke: Palgrave Macmillan, 2011).

Stirk, Peter M. R. (ed.), *European Unity in Context: The Interwar Period* (London: Bloomsbury, 2016).

Stråth, Bo, *Europe's Utopias of Peace: 1815, 1919, 1951* (London: Bloomsbury, 2016).

Vayssière, Bertrand, *Vers une Europe fédérale? Les espoirs et les actions fédéralistes au sortir de la seconde guerre mondiale* (Brussels: Peter Lang, 2006).

Weller, Shane, *The Idea of Europe: A Critical History* (Cambridge: Cambridge University Press, 2021).

Wintle, Michael J., *Eurocentrism: History, Identity, White Man's Burden* (London: Routledge, 2020).

B.4 The Context: European History since 1945

Ash, Timothy Garton, *Homelands: A Personal History of Europe* (London: The Bodley Head, 2023).

Berend, Ivan T., *An Economic History of Twentieth-Century Europe: Economic Regimes from Laissez-Faire to Globalization* (Cambridge: Cambridge University Press, 2006).

Conway, Martin, *Western Europe's Democratic Age, 1945–1968* (Princeton, NJ: Princeton University Press, 2020).

Eichengreen, Barry, *The European Economy since 1945: Coordinated Capitalism and Beyond* (Princeton, NJ: Princeton University Press, 2007).

Jarausch, Konrad H., *Embattled Europe: A Progressive Alternative* (Princeton, NJ: Princeton University Press, 2021).

Jarausch, Konrad H., *Out of Ashes: A New History of Europe in the Twentieth Century* (Princeton, NJ: Princeton University Press, 2015).

Bibliographical Essay

Judt, Tony, *Postwar: A History of Europe since 1945* (London: Pimlico, 2007).

Kaelble, Hartmut, *A Social History of Europe, 1945–2000: Recovery and Transformation after Two World Wars* (New York: Berghahn, 2013).

Kershaw, Ian, *Roller-Coaster: Europe, 1950–2017* (London: Allen Lane, 2018).

Kott, Sandrine, *A World More Equal: An Internationalist Perspective on the Cold War* (New York: Columbia University Press, 2024).

Sarotte, Mary E., *1989: The Struggle to Create Post-Cold War Europe* (Princeton, NJ: Princeton University Press, 2014).

Schot, Johan and Philip Scranton (eds.), *Making Europe: Technology and Transformations, 1850–2000*, 6 vols. (New York: Palgrave Macmillan, 2013–2019).

Stone, Dan (ed.), *The Oxford Handbook of Postwar European History* (Oxford: Oxford University Press, 2012).

Ther, Philipp, *Das andere Ende der Geschichte: Über die Große Transformation* (Berlin: Suhrkamp, 2019).

Ther, Philipp, *Europe since 1989: A History* (Princeton, NJ: Princeton University Press, 2016).

Tooze, Adam, *Crashed: How a Decade of Financial Crises Changed the World* (New York: Allen Lane, 2018).

B.5 Syntheses and Overviews of EU History

Anderson, Perry, *Ever Closer Union? Europe in the West* (London: Verso, 2021).

Dinan, Desmond, *Europe Recast: A History of European Union*. 2nd ed. (Basingstoke: Palgrave Macmillan, 2014).

Dinan, Desmond (ed.), *Origins and Evolution of the European Union*. 2nd ed. (Oxford: Oxford University Press, 2014).

Gehler, Michael (ed.), *From Common Market to European Union Building: 50 Years of the Rome Treaties 1957–2007* (Vienna: Böhlau, 2009).

Gilbert, Mark, *European Integration: A Political History*. 2nd ed. (Lanham, MD: Rowman & Littlefield, 2021).

Hewitson, Mark, *European Integration since the 1920s: Security, Identity, and Cooperation* (Oxford: Oxford University Press, 2024).

Kaelble, Hartmut, *Der verkannte Bürger: Eine andere Geschichte der europäischen Integration seit 1950* (Frankfurt am Main: Campus, 2019).

Leucht, Brigitte, Katja Seidel and Laurent Warlouzet (eds.), *Reinventing Europe: The History of the European Union since 1945* (London: Bloomsbury, 2023).

Loth, Wilfried, *Building Europe: A History of European Unification* (Berlin: De Gruyter, 2015).

Meurs, Wim van, et al., *The Unfinished History of European Integration*. 2nd, revised ed. (Amsterdam: Amsterdam University Press, 2024).

Middelaar, Luuk van, *The Passage to Europe: How a Continent Became a Union* (New Haven, CT: Yale University Press, 2013).

Patel, Kiran Klaus, *Project Europe: A History* (Cambridge: Cambridge University Press, 2020).

Pinder, John and Simon Usherwood, *The European Union: A Very Short Introduction*. 4th ed. (Oxford: Oxford University Press, 2018).

Schulz-Forberg, Hagen and Bo Stråth, *The Political History of European Integration: The Hypocrisy of Democracy-through-Market* (London: Routledge, 2010).

Segers, Mathieu and Steven Van Hecke (eds.), *The Cambridge History of the European Union*, 2 vols. (Cambridge: Cambridge University Press, 2024).

Warlouzet, Laurent, *Europe contre Europe: Entre liberté, solidarité et puissance* (Paris: CNRS Éditions, 2022).

B.6 Conceptional Questions and Historiography

Gehler, Michael and Silvio Vietta (eds.), *Europa – Europäisierung – Europäistik: Neue wissenschaftliche Ansätze, Methoden und Inhalte* (Vienna: Böhlau, 2010).

Gerbet, Pierre, Gérard Bossuat and Thierry Grosbois, *Dictionnaire historique de l'Europe unie* (Brussels: André Versaille, 2009).

Gilbert, Mark, 'Historicising European Integration History', in: *European Review of International Studies* 8 (2021), 221–240.

Gilbert, Mark, 'Narrating the Process: Questioning the Progressive Story of European Integration', in: *Journal of Common Market Studies* 46 (2008), 641–662.

Heumen, Lennaert van and Mechthild Roos (eds.), *The Informal Construction of Europe* (London: Routledge, 2019).

Kaiser, Wolfram and Antonio Varsori (eds.), *European Union History: Themes and Debates* (Houndmills: Palgrave Macmillan, 2010).

Laursen, Finn, *Historical Dictionary of the European Union* (Lanham, MD: Rowman & Littlefield, 2016).

Moreno Juste, Antonio, 'La incierta levedad de la europeización: Una mirada desde los estudios europeos y su impacto sobre la agenda del historiador', in: *Vínculos de Historia* 13 (2024), 93–114.

Mourlon-Druol, Emmanuel, 'Rich, Vivid, and Ignored: History in European Studies', in: *Politique européenne* 50 (2015), 56–69.

Ostrowski, Marius S., 'Europeanism: A Historical View', in: *Contemporary European History* 32 (2023), 287–304.

Patel, Kiran Klaus, 'Provincialising European Union: Co-operation and Integration in Europe in a Historical Perspective', in: *Contemporary European History* 22 (2013), 649–673.

Patel, Kiran Klaus, 'Widening and Deepening? Recent Advances in European Integration History', in: *Neue Politische Literatur* 64 (2019), 327–357.

Petrini, Francesco, 'Integrazione e conflitto: Per una storia materialista della costruzione europea', in: *Ventunesimo Secolo* 48 (2021), 10–35.

Romano, Angela, 'Parallelism, Asymmetry and Convergence in Cold War Europe', in: *Politique européenne* 76 (2022), 146–172.

Warlouzet, Laurent, 'Dépasser la crise de l'histoire de l'intégration européenne', in: *Politique européenne* 44 (2014), 98–122.
Wiener, Antje, Tanja A. Börzel and Thomas Risse (eds.), *European Integration Theory*. 3rd ed. (Oxford: Oxford University Press, 2019).

B.7 European Integration during the Cold War

Bickerton, Christopher J., *European Integration: From Nation-States to Member-States* (Oxford: Oxford University Press, 2012).
Bozo, Frédéric, et al. (eds.), *Visions of the End of the Cold War in Europe, 1945–1990* (New York: Berghahn Books, 2012).
Bussière, Éric, et al. (eds.), *The European Commission 1973–86: History and Memories of an Institution* (Luxembourg: Publications Office of the European Union, 2014).
Deighton, Anne and Alan S. Milward (eds.), *Widening, Deepening and Acceleration: The European Economic Community 1957–1963* (Baden-Baden: Nomos, 1999).
Dumoulin, Michel (ed.), *The European Commission, 1958–72: History and Memories* (Luxembourg: Office for Official Publications of the European Communities, 2007).
Duranti, Marco, *The Conservative Human Rights Revolution: European Identity, Transnational Politics, and the Origins of the European Convention* (Oxford: Oxford University Press, 2017).
Gehler, Michael and Wilfried Loth (eds.), *Reshaping Europe: Towards a Political, Economic and Monetary Union, 1984–1989* (Baden-Baden: Nomos, 2020).
Gehler, Michael and Wolfram Kaiser (eds.), *Transnationale Parteienkooperation der europäischen Christdemokraten: Dokumente 1945–1965* (Munich: Saur, 2004).
Gillingham, John, *Coal, Steel, and the Rebirth of Europe, 1945–1955: The Germans and French from Ruhr Conflict to Economic Community* (Cambridge: Cambridge University Press, 1991).

Harst, Jan van der (ed.), *Beyond the Customs Union: The European Community's Quest for Deepening, Widening and Completion, 1969–1975* (Brussels: Bruylant, 2007).

Hiepel, Claudia (ed.), *Europe in a Globalising World: Global Challenges and European Responses in the 'Long' 1970s* (Baden-Baden: Nomos, 2014).

Kaiser, Wolfram, *Shaping European Union: The European Parliament and Institutional Reform, 1979–1989* (Brussels: European Union, 2018).

Kaiser, Wolfram and Jürgen Elvert (eds.), *European Union Enlargement: A Comparative History* (London: Routledge, 2004).

Kaiser, Wolfram, Brigitte Leucht and Morten Rasmussen (eds.), *The History of the European Union: Origins of a Trans- and Supranational Polity 1950–72* (London: Routledge, 2008).

Kaiser, Wolfram and Jan-Henrik Meyer (eds.), *Societal Actors in European Integration: Polity-Building and Policy-Making 1958–1992* (Basingstoke: Palgrave Macmillan, 2013).

Knipping, Franz and Matthias Schönwald (eds.), *Aufbruch zum Europa der zweiten Generation: Die europäische Einigung 1969–1984* (Trier: Wissenschaftlicher Verlag Trier, 2004).

Laursen, Johnny (ed.), *The Institutions and Dynamics of the European Community, 1973–83* (Baden-Baden: Nomos, 2014).

Lipgens, Walter, *Die Anfänge der europäischen Einigungspolitik 1945–1950*, 2 vols. (Stuttgart: Ernst Klett Verlag, 1977).

Loth, Wilfried (ed.), *Crises and Compromises: The European Project 1963–69* (Baden-Baden: Nomos, 2001).

Ludlow, N. Piers, *The European Community and the Crises of the 1960s: Negotiating the Gaullist Challenge* (London: Routledge, 2006).

Ludlow, N. Piers (ed.), *European Integration and the Cold War: Ostpolitik–Westpolitik, 1965–1973* (London: Routledge, 2007).

Ludlow, N. Piers, *Roy Jenkins and the European Commission Presidency 1976–1980: At the Heart of Europe* (Basingstoke: Palgrave Macmillan, 2016).

Miard-Delacroix, Hélène, *Im Zeichen der europäischen Einigung: 1963 bis in die Gegenwart* (Darmstadt: WBG, 2011).

Milward, Alan S., *The European Rescue of the Nation-State*, 2nd ed. (London: Routledge, 2000).

Milward, Alan S., *The Reconstruction of Western Europe, 1945–51* (Berkeley: University of California Press, 1984).

Palayret, Jean-Marie, Helen Wallace and Pascaline Winand (eds.), *Visions, Votes and Vetoes: The Empty Chair Crisis and the Luxembourg Compromise Forty Years On* (Brussels: Lang, 2006).

Pistone, Sergio, *The Union of European Federalists: From the Foundation to the Decision on Direct Election of the European Parliament (1946–1974)* (Milan: Giuffrè, 2008).

Romano, Angela and Federico Romero (eds.), *European Socialist Regime's Fateful Engagement with the West: National Strategies in the Long 1970s* (London: Routledge, 2021).

Rosato, Sebastian, *Europe United: Power Politics and the Making of the European Community* (Ithaca, NY: Cornell University Press, 2011).

Schain, Martin (ed.), *The Marshall Plan: Fifty Years After* (New York: Palgrave Macmillan, 2001).

Thomas, Daniel C., *The Helsinki Effect: International Norms, Human Rights, and the Demise of Communism* (Princeton: Princeton University Press, 2001).

Trausch, Gilbert (ed.), *Die europäische Integration vom Schuman-Plan bis zu den Verträgen von Rom* (Baden-Baden: Nomos, 1993).

Vanke, Jeffrey, *Europeanism and European Union: Interests, Emotions, and Systemic Integration into the Early Economic Community* (Palo Alto, CA: Academica Press, 2010).

Varsori, Antonio (ed.), *Alle origini del presente: L'Europa occidentale nella crisi degli anni Settanta* (Milan: FrancoAngeli, 2007).

Varsori, Antonio (ed.), *Inside the European Community: Actors and Policies in the European Integration 1957–1972* (Baden-Baden: Nomos, 2006).

Warlouzet, Laurent, *Governing Europe in a Globalizing World: Neoliberalism and Its Alternatives Following the 1973 Oil Crisis* (London: Routledge, 2018).

Weiler, Joseph H. H., *The Constitution of Europe: 'Do the New Clothes Have an Emperor?' and Other Essays on European Integration* (Cambridge: Cambridge University Press, 1999).

Wilkens, Andreas (ed.), *Le plan Schuman dans l'histoire: Intérêts nationaux et projet européen* (Brussels: Bruylant, 2004).

B.8 European Integration since the End of the Cold War

Arnull, Anthony and Damian Chalmers (eds.), *The Oxford Handbook of European Union Law* (Oxford: Oxford University Press, 2015).

Barber, N. W., Maria Cahill and Richard Ekins (eds.), *The Rise and Fall of the European Constitution* (London: Hart, 2019).

Bozo, Frédéric, et al. (eds.), *Europe and the End of the Cold War: A Reappraisal* (London: Routledge, 2008).

Coman, Ramona, Amandine Crespy and Vivien Schmidt (eds.), *Governance and Politics in the Post-Crisis European Union* (Cambridge: Cambridge University Press, 2020).

Dinan, Desmond, Neill Nugent and William E. Paterson (eds.), *The European Union in Crisis* (London: Palgrave, 2017).

Dujardin, Vincent, et al. (eds.), *The European Commission 1986–2000: History and Memories of an Institution* (Luxembourg: Publications Office of the European Union, 2019).

Dyson, Kenneth and Ivo Maes (eds.), *Architects of the Euro: Intellectuals in the Making of the European Monetary Union* (Oxford: Oxford University Press, 2016).

Dyson, Kenneth and Kevin Featherstone, *The Road to Maastricht: Negotiating Economic and Monetary Union* (Oxford: Oxford University Press, 1999).

Faure, Samuel and Christian Lequesne (eds.), *The Elgar Companion to the European Union* (Cheltenham: Edward Elgar, 2023).

Ferrera, Maurizio, *The Boundaries of Welfare: European Integration and the New Spatial Politics of Social Protection* (Oxford: Oxford University Press, 2005).

Hodson, Dermot and Imelda Maher, *The Transformation of EU Treaty Making: The Rise of Parliaments, Referendums and Courts since 1950* (Cambridge: Cambridge University Press, 2018).

Hutter, Swen, Edgar Grande and Hanspeter Kriesi (eds.), *Politicising Europe: Integration and Mass Politics* (Cambridge: Cambridge University Press, 2016).

Jones, Erik, Anand Menon and Stephen Weatherill (eds.), *The Oxford Handbook of the European Union* (Oxford: Oxford University Press, 2012).

Jørgensen, Knud Erik, Mark Pollack and Ben Rosamond (eds.), *The SAGE Handbook of European Union Politics* (London: SAGE, 2006).

Kohler-Koch, Beate and Berthold Rittberger (eds.), *Debating the Democratic Legitimacy of the European Union* (Lanham, MD: Rowman & Littlefield, 2007).

Krastev, Ivan, *After Europe*. Updated ed. (Philadelphia: University of Pennsylvania Press, 2020).

Laczó, Ferenc and Luka Lisjak Gabrijelčič, *The Legacy of Division: East and West after 1989* (Budapest: CEU Press, 2020).

Landesmann, Michael and István P. Székely (eds.), *Does EU Membership Facilitate Convergence? The Experience of the EU's Eastern Enlargement* (Basingstoke: Palgrave Macmillan, 2021).

Mayhew, Alan, *Recreating Europe: The European Union's Policy towards Central and Eastern Europe* (Cambridge: Cambridge University Press, 1998).

Middelaar, Luuk van, *Alarums and Excursions: Improvising Politics on the European Stage* (Newcastle upon Tyne: Agenda Publishing, 2019).

Neunreither, Karlheinz and Antje Wiener (eds.), *European Integration after Amsterdam: Institutional Dynamics and Prospects for Democracy* (Oxford: Oxford University Press, 2000).

Phinnemore, David, *The Treaty of Lisbon: Origins and Negotiation* (Basingstoke: Palgrave Macmillan, 2013).

Piattoni, Simona (ed.), *The European Union: Democratic Principles and Institutional Architectures in Times of Crisis* (Oxford: Oxford University Press, 2015).

Vollaard, Hans, *European Disintegration: A Search for Explanations* (London: Palgrave Macmillan, 2018).

Williams, Andrew, *EU Human Rights Policies: A Study in Irony* (Oxford: Oxford University Press, 2004).

Wirsching, Andreas, *Der Preis der Freiheit: Geschichte Europas in unserer Zeit* (Munich: Beck, 2011).

Zielonka, Jan, *Counter-Revolution: Liberal Europe in Retreat* (Oxford: Oxford University Press, 2018).

Zyla, Benjamin, *The End of European Security Institutions? The EU's Common Foreign Security Policy and NATO after Brexit* (Cham: Springer, 2020).

B.9 Specific (Former) Member States

Andor, László, *Hungary on the Road to the European Union: Transition in Blue* (Westport, CT: Praeger, 2000).

Bakó, Beáta, *Challenges to EU Values in Hungary: How the European Union Misunderstood the Government of Viktor Orbán* (London: Routledge, 2023).

Bogdandy, Armin von and Pál Sonnevend (eds.), *Constitutional Crisis in the European Constitutional Area: Theory, Law and Politics in Hungary and Romania* (Oxford: Hart, 2015).

Bossuat, Gérard, *La France et la construction de l'unité européenne: de 1919 à nos jours* (Paris: Colin, 2012).

Bozo, Frédéric, *Mitterrand, the End of the Cold War, and German Unification* (New York: Berghahn, 2009).

Cordell, Karl (ed.), *Poland and the European Union* (London: Routledge, 2000).

Craveri, Piero and Antonio Varsori (eds.), *L'Italia nella costruzione europea: Un bilancio storico (1957–2007)* (Milan: FrancoAngeli, 2009).

D'Ottavio, Gabriele, *Europa mit den Deutschen: Die Bundesrepublik und die europäische Integration (1949–1966)* (Berlin: Duncker & Humblot, 2016).

Diez, Thomas (ed.), *The European Union and the Cyprus Conflict: Modern Conflict, Postmodern Union* (Manchester: Manchester University Press, 2002).

Dimitrakopoulos, Dionyssis G. and Argyris G. Passas (eds.), *Greece in the European Union* (London: Routledge, 2004).

Ellison, James, *Threatening Europe: Britain and the Creation of the European Community, 1955–58* (Basingstoke: Macmillan, 2000).
Ferreira-Pereira, Laura C. (ed.), *Portugal in the European Union: Assessing Twenty-Five Years of Integration Experience* (London: Routledge, 2014).
Gehler, Michael, *Der lange Weg nach Europa: Österreich vom Ende der Monarchie bis zur EU* (Vienna: StudienVerlag, 2002).
Gehler, Michael and Maximilian Graf (eds.), *Europa und die deutsche Einheit: Beobachtungen, Entscheidungen und Folgen* (Göttingen: Vandenhoeck & Ruprecht, 2017).
Graziano, Paolo Roberto, *Europeanization and Domestic Policy Change: The Case of Italy* (London: Routledge, 2013).
Grob-Fitzgibbon, Benjamin, *Continental Drift: Britain and Europe from the End of Empire to the Rise of Euroscepticism* (Cambridge: Cambridge University Press, 2016).
Guirao, Fernando, *The European Rescue of the Franco Regime, 1950–1975* (Oxford: Oxford University Press, 2021).
Guirao, Fernando, *Spain and the Reconstruction of Western Europe, 1945–1957: Challenge and Response* (New York: St. Martin's Press, 1998).
Haeussler, Mathias, *Helmut Schmidt and British–German Relations: A European Misunderstanding* (Cambridge: Cambridge University Press, 2019).
Harryvan, Anjo G., *In Pursuit of Influence: The Netherlands' European Policy during the Formative Years of the European Union, 1952–1973* (Brussels: Peter Lang, 2009).
Harwood, Mark, *Malta in the European Union* (Abingdon: Routledge, 2014).
Jacobsson, Bengt, *The European Union and the Baltic States: Changing Forms of Governance* (London: Routledge, 2010).
Karamouzi, Eirini, *Greece, the EEC and the Cold War, 1974–1979: The Second Enlargement* (Basingstoke: Palgrave Macmillan, 2014).
Katsikas, Stefanos (ed.), *Bulgaria and Europe: Shifting Identities* (London: Anthem Press, 2010).
Krotz, Ulrich and Joachim Schild, *Shaping Europe: France, Germany, and Embedded Bilateralism from the Elysée Treaty*

to Twenty-First Century Politics (Oxford: Oxford University Press, 2013).

Laffan, Brigid and Jane O'Mahony, *Ireland and the European Union* (Basingstoke: Palgrave Macmillan, 2008).

Magone, José M., *The Developing Place of Portugal in the European Union* (Abingdon: Routledge, 2004).

Maldini, Pero and Davor Pauković (eds.), *Croatia and the European Union: Changes and Development* (London: Routledge, 2015).

Marti, Simon, *Schweizer Europapolitik am Wendepunkt: Interessen, Konzepte und Entscheidungsprozesse in den Verhandlungen über den Europäischen Wirtschaftsraum* (Baden-Baden: Nomos, 2013).

Marek, Dan and Michael J. Baun, *The Czech Republic and the European Union* (London: Routledge, 2011).

Miles, Lee (ed.), *Fusing with Europe? Sweden in the European Union* (London: Routledge, 2005).

Miles, Lee and Anders Wivel (eds.), *Denmark and the European Union* (London: Routledge, 2014).

Mole, Richard, *The Baltic States from the Soviet Union to the European Union: Identity, Discourse and Power in the Post-Communist Transition of Estonia, Latvia and Lithuania* (London: Routledge, 2012).

Mrak, Mojmir, Matija Rojec and Carlos Silva-Jáuregui (eds.), *Slovenia: From Yugoslavia to the European Union* (Washington, DC: World Bank, 2004).

Olesen, Thorsten B. (ed.), *Interdependence versus Integration: Denmark, Scandinavia and Western Europe, 1945–1960* (Odense: Odense University Press, 1995).

Paoli, Simone, *Frontiera Sud: L'Italia e la nascita dell'Europa di Schengen* (Florence: Le Monnier, 2018).

Papadimitriou, Dimitris and David Phinnemore, *Romania and the European Union: From Marginalisation to Membership* (London: Routledge, 2008).

Patel, Kiran Klaus (ed.), *Tangled Transformations: Unifying Germany and Integrating Europe, 1985–1995* (Toronto: University of Toronto Press, 2024).

Patel, Kiran Klaus and Kenneth Weisbrode (eds.), *European Integration and the Atlantic Community in the 1980s* (Cambridge: Cambridge University Press, 2013).

Pinto, António Costa and Nuno Severiano Teixeira (eds.), *Southern Europe and the Making of the European Union 1945–1980s* (New York: Columbia University Press, 2002).

Raunio, Tapio and Teija Tiilikainen, *Finland in the European Union* (London: Frank Cass, 2003).

Royo, Sebastián and Paul Christopher Manuel (eds.), *Spain and Portugal in the European Union: The First Fifteen Years* (London: Frank Cass, 2003).

Saunders, Robert, *Yes to Europe! The 1975 Referendum and Seventies Britain* (Cambridge: Cambridge University Press, 2018).

Schwabe, Klaus, *Jean Monnet: Frankreich, die Deutschen und die Einigung Europas* (Baden-Baden: Nomos, 2016).

Segers, Mathieu, *The Netherlands and European Integration, 1950 to Present* (Amsterdam: Amsterdam University Press, 2020).

Teixeira, Nuno Severiano and António Costa Pinto (eds.), *The Europeanization of Portuguese Democracy* (New York: Columbia University Press, 2012).

Varsori, Antonio, *La Cenerentola d'Europa? L'Italia e l'integrazione europea dal 1947 a oggi* (Soveria Mannelli: Rubbettino, 2010).

Vollaard, Hans, Jan Beyers and Patrick Dumont (eds.), *European Integration and Consensus Politics in the Low Countries* (London: Routledge, 2015).

Wall, Stephen, *Reluctant European: Britain and the European Union from 1945 to Brexit* (Oxford: Oxford University Press, 2020).

Warlouzet, Laurent, *Le choix de la CEE par la France: L'Europe économique en débat de Mendès France à de Gaulle, 1955–1969* (Paris: CHEFF, 2011).

Zaccaria, Benedetto, *The EEC's Yugoslav Policy in Cold War Europe, 1968–1980* (Basingstoke: Palgrave Macmillan, 2016).

B.10 Policy Fields, EU Law, Representation and Contestation

Albors-Llorens, Albertina, Catherine Barnard and Brigitte Leucht (eds.), *Cassis de Dijon: 40 Years On* (London: Bloomsbury Publishing, 2021).

Andry, Aurélie Dianara, *Social Europe, the Road Not Taken: The Left and European Integration in the Long 1970s* (Oxford: Oxford University Press, 2022).

Brunnermeier, Markus K., Harold James and Jean-Pierre Landau, *The Euro and the Battle of Ideas* (Princeton: Princeton University Press, 2016).

Bussière, Éric, *L'Europe de Jacques Delors: Gestation et mise en oeuvre d'un projet* (Paris: Sorbonne Université Presses, 2024).

Bussière, Éric, Michel Dumoulin and Sylvain Schirmann (eds.), *Milieux économiques et intégration européenne au XXe siècle: La relance des années quatre-vingt (1979–1992)* (Paris: Institut de la gestion publique et du développement économique, 2007).

Coppolaro, Lucia, *The Making of a World Trading Power: The European Economic Community (EEC) in the GATT Kennedy Round Negotiations (1963–67)* (Farnham: Ashgate, 2013).

Corbett, Richard et al., *Shaping European Integration: The Directly Elected European Parliament 1979–1989* (Luxembourg: EPRS, 2024).

Crespy, Amandine, *The European Social Question: Tackling Key Controversies* (Newcastle: Agenda, 2022).

Dumoulin, Michel, Pierre Guillen and Maurice Vaïsse (eds.), *L'énergie nucléaire en Europe: Des origines à Euratom* (Bern: Peter Lang, 1994).

Găinar, Maria and Martial Libera (eds.), *Contre l'Europe? Anti-européisme, euroscepticisme et alter-européisme dans la construction européenne de 1945 à nos jours* (Stuttgart: Franz Steiner Verlag, 2013).

Guerrieri, Sandro, *Un Parlamento oltre le nazioni: L'Assemblea Comune della CECA e le sfide dell'integrazione europea (1952–1958)* (Bologna: Il Mulino, 2016).
Hofmann, Stephanie C., *European Security in NATO's Shadow: Party Ideologies and Institution Building* (Cambridge: Cambridge University Press, 2013).
James, Harold, *Making the European Monetary Union: The Role of the Committee of Central Bank Governors and the Origins of the European Central Bank* (Cambridge, MA: Belknap Press, 2012).
Jordan, Andrew and Viviane Gravey (eds.), *Environmental Policy in the EU: Actors, Institutions and Processes* (London: Routledge, 2021).
Kaeding, Michael, Johannes Pollak and Paul Schmidt (eds.), *Euroscepticism and the Future of Europe: Views from the Capitals* (Cham: Palgrave Macmillan, 2021).
Kaiser, Wolfram, *Christian Democracy and the Origins of European Union* (Cambridge: Cambridge University Press, 2007).
Knudsen, Ann-Christina L., *Farmers on Welfare: The Making of Europe's Common Agricultural Policy* (Ithaca, NY: Cornell University Press, 2009).
Leruth, Benjamin, Nicholas Startin and Simon Usherwood (eds.), *The Routledge Handbook of Euroscepticism* (London: Routledge, 2018).
Marsh, David, *The Euro: The Politics of the New Global Currency* (New Haven, CT: Yale University Press, 2009).
Mitzner, Veera, *European Union Research Policy: Contested Origins* (Cham: Palgrave Macmillan, 2020).
Mourlon-Druol, Emmanuel, *A Europe Made of Money: The Emergence of the European Monetary System* (Ithaca, NY: Cornell University Press, 2012).
Moyn, Samuel, *The Last Utopia: Human Rights in History* (Cambridge, MA: Belknap Press of Harvard University Press, 2010).
Nicola, Fernanda and Bill Davies (eds.), *EU Law Stories: Contextual and Critical Histories of European Jurisprudence* (Cambridge: Cambridge University Press, 2017).

Pasquinucci, Daniele and Luca Verzichelli (eds.), *Contro l'Europa? I diversi scetticismi verso l'integrazione europea* (Bologna: Il Mulino, 2016).
Patel, Kiran Klaus (ed.), *The Cultural Politics of Europe: European Capitals of Culture and European Union since the 1980s* (London: Routledge, 2013).
Patel, Kiran Klaus (ed.), *Fertile Ground for Europe? The History of European Integration and the Common Agricultural Policy since 1945* (Baden-Baden: Nomos, 2009).
Patel, Kiran Klaus and Heike Schweitzer (eds.), *The Historical Foundations of EU Competition Law* (Oxford: Oxford University Press, 2013).
Pomfret, Richard W. T., *The Economic Integration of Europe* (Cambridge, MA: Harvard University Press, 2021).
Rittberger, Berthold, *Building Europe's Parliament: Democratic Representation beyond the Nation State* (Oxford: Oxford University Press, 2005).
Schorkopf, Frank, *Die unentschiedene Macht: Verfassungsgeschichte der Europäischen Union, 1948–2007* (Göttingen: Vandenhoeck & Ruprecht, 2023).
Stanley-Becker, Isaac, *Europe without Borders: A History* (Princeton: Princeton University Press, 2025).
Sternberg, Claudia, *The Struggle for EU Legitimacy: Public Contestation, 1950–2005* (Basingstoke: Palgrave Macmillan, 2013).
Varsori, Antonio (ed.), *Sfide del mercato e identità europea: Le politiche di educazione e formazione professionale nell'Europa comunitaria* (Milan: FrancoAngeli, 2006).
Vauchez, Antoine, *Brokering Europe: Euro-Lawyers and the Making of a Transnational Polity* (Cambridge: Cambridge University Press, 2015).
Wassenberg, Birte, Frédéric Clavert and Philippe Hamman (eds.), *Contre l'Europe? Anti-européisme, euroscepticisme et alter-européisme dans la construction européenne de 1945 à nos jours* (Stuttgart: Franz Steiner Verlag, 2010).
Wessels, Wolfgang, *Die Öffnung des Staates: Modelle und Wirklichkeit grenzüberschreitender Verwaltungspraxis* (Wiesbaden: Leske + Budrich, 2000).

B.11 European Integration and the Wider World

Albers, Martin, *Britain, France, West Germany and the People's Republic of China, 1969–1982: The European Dimension of China's Great Transition* (London: Palgrave Macmillan, 2016).

Archer, Clive, *Norway Outside the European Union: Norway and European Integration from 1994 to 2004* (Abingdon: Routledge, 2005).

Aubourg, Valérie, Gérard Bossuat and Giles Scott-Smith (eds.), *European Community, Atlantic Community?* (Paris: Soleb, 2008).

Bitsch, Marie-Thérèse and Gérard Bossuat (eds.), *L'Europe unie et l'Afrique: De l'idée d'Eurafrique à la convention de Lomé I* (Brussels: Bruylant, 2005).

Bitumi, Alessandra, Gabriele D'Ottavio and Giuliana Laschi (eds.), *La Comunità europea e le relazioni esterne 1957–1992* (Bologna: CLUEB, 2008).

Borzenko, Olena Oleksandrivna (eds.), *Otsinka intehratsii Ukraïny do Ievropeis'koho ekonomichnoho prostoru: Kolektyvna monohrafia* (Kyiv: NAN Ukraïny, DU Instytut ekonomiki ta prohnozuvannia NAN Ukraïny, 2021).

Bossuat, Gérard and Nicolas Vaicbourdt (eds.), *Etats-Unis, Europe et Union européenne: Histoire et avenir d'un partenariat difficile (1945–1999)* (Brussels: Peter Lang, 2001).

Bradford, Anu, *The Brussels Effect: How the European Union Rules the World* (Oxford: Oxford University Press, 2020).

Buettner, Elizabeth, *Europe after Empire: Decolonization, Society and Culture* (Cambridge: Cambridge University Press, 2016).

Casarini, Nicola, *Remaking Global Order: The Evolution of Europe-China Relations and Its Implications for East Asia and the United States* (Oxford: Oxford University Press, 2009).

Church, Clive H. (ed.), *Switzerland and the European Union: A Close, Contradictory and Misunderstood Relationship* (London: Routledge, 2006).

Dimier, Véronique, *The Invention of a European Development Aid Bureaucracy: Recycling Empire* (Basingstoke: Palgrave Macmillan, 2014).

Dykmann, Klaas, *Perceptions and Politics: The Foreign Relations of the European Union with Latin America* (Madrid: Iberoamericana Vervuert, 2006).

Ferrari, Lorenzo, *Sometimes Speaking with a Single Voice: The European Community as an International Actor, 1969–1979* (Brussels: Peter Lang, 2016).

Ferreira-Pereira, Laura C. and Michael Smith (eds.), *The European Union's Strategic Partnerships: Global Diplomacy in a Contested World* (Cham: Palgrave Macmillan, 2021).

Frattolillo, Oliviero, *Diplomacy in Japan-EU Relations: From the Cold War to the Post-Bipolar Era* (London: Routledge, 2013).

Găinar, Maria, *Aux origines de la diplomatie européenne: Les Neuf et la Coopération politique européenne de 1973 à 1980* (Brussels: Peter Lang, 2012).

Garavini, Giuliano, *After Empires: European Integration, Decolonization, and the Challenge from the Global South, 1957–1985* (Oxford: Oxford University Press, 2012).

Gehler, Michael and Rolf Steininger (eds.), *Die Neutralen und die europäische Integration, 1945–1995* (Vienna: Böhlau, 2000).

Giauque, Jeffrey Glen, *Grand Designs and Visions of Unity: The Atlantic Powers and the Reorganization of Western Europe, 1955–1963* (Chapel Hill, NC: University of North Carolina Press, 2002).

Hansen, Peo and Stefan Jonsson, *Eurafrica: The Untold History of European Integration and Colonialism* (London: Bloomsbury, 2014).

Johnson, Debra and Paul Robinson (eds.), *Perspectives on EU–Russia Relations* (London: Routledge, 2005).

Jørgensen, Knud Erik, et al. (eds.), *The SAGE Handbook of European Foreign Policy* (Los Angeles, CA: SAGE, 2015).

Keck, Jörn, Dimitri Vanoverbeke and Franz Waldenberger (eds.), *EU-Japan Relations, 1970–2012: From Confrontation to Global Partnership* (London: Routledge, 2013).

Krotz, Ulrich, Kiran Klaus Patel and Federico Romero (eds.), *Europe's Cold War Relations: The EC Towards a Global Role* (London: Bloomsbury, 2020).

Leruth, Benjamin, Stefan Gänzle and Jarle Trondal (eds.), *The Routledge Handbook of Differentiation in the European Union* (Milton: Routledge, 2022).

Lévi Coral, Michel, *La Unión Europea y América Latina: Relaciones entre bloques regionales e integración regional* (Quito: Universidad Andina Simón Bolivar, 2014).

Lundestad, Geir, *The United States and Western Europe since 1945: From 'Empire' by Invitation to Transatlantic Drift* (Oxford: Oxford University Press, 2003).

Meijer, Hugo, *Awakening to China's Rise: European Foreign Policy and Security Policies toward the People's Republic of China* (New York: Oxford University Press, 2022).

Möckli, Daniel, *European Foreign Policy during the Cold War: Heath, Brandt, Pompidou and the Dream of Political Unity* (London: I. B. Tauris, 2009).

Montarsolo, Yves, *L'Eurafrique, contrepoint de l'idée d'Europe: Le cas français de la fin de la deuxième guerre mondiale aux négociations* (Aix-en-Provence: Publications de l'Université de Provence, 2010).

Mourlon-Druol, Emmanuel and Federico Romero (eds.), *International Summitry and Global Governance: The Rise of the G7 and the European Council, 1974–1991* (London: Routledge, 2014).

Neuss, Beate, *Geburtshelfer Europas? Die Rolle der Vereinigten Staaten im europäischen Integrationsprozeß 1945–1958* (Baden-Baden: Nomos, 2000).

Nicolaïdis, Kalypso, Berny Sèbe and Gabrielle Maas (eds.), *Echoes of Empire: Memory, Identity and Colonial Legacies* (London: I. B. Tauris, 2015).

Rempe, Martin, *Entwicklung im Konflikt: Die EWG und der Senegal 1957–1975* (Cologne: Böhlau, 2012).

Rothacher, Albrecht, *Economic Diplomacy between the European Community and Japan, 1959–1981* (Aldershot: Gower, 1983).

Roy, Joaquín, José María Lladós and Félix Peña (eds.), *Después d Santiago: Integración regional y relaciones Unión Europea – América Latina* (Miami, FL: Thomson-Shore, 2013).

Schulz, Matthias and Thomas A. Schwartz (eds.), *The Strained Alliance: U.S.-European Relations from Nixon to Carter* (Cambridge: Cambridge University Press, 2010).

Scott-Smith, Giles and Valérie Aubourg (eds.), *Atlantic, Euratlantic, or Europe-America?* (Paris: Soleb, 2011).

Trachtenberg, Marc, *A Constructed Peace: The Making of the European Settlement, 1945–1963* (Princeton, NJ: Princeton University Press, 1999).

Uğur, Mehmet and Nergis Canefe (eds.), *Turkey and European Integration: Accession Prospects and Issues* (London: Routledge, 2004).

Vahsen, Urban, *Eurafrikanische Entwicklungskooperation: Die Assoziierungspolitik der EWG gegenüber dem subsaharischen Afrika in den 1960er Jahren* (Stuttgart: Franz Steiner Verlag, 2010).

Varsori, Antonio and Guia Migani (eds.), *Europe in the International Arena during the 1970s: Entering a Different World* (Brussels: Peter Lang, 2011).

Winand, Pascaline, Andrea Benvenuti and Max Guderzo (eds.), *The External Relations of the European Union: Historical and Contemporary Perspectives* (Brussels: Peter Lang, 2015).

INDEX

acquis communautaire, 63, 132, 152, 165, 188
Adenauer, Konrad, 21, 28, 30, 58
Africa, 8–9, 109, 155, 168. *See also* association with the EC/EU; Lomé Convention; Yaoundé Convention
  colonialism, 11, 35, 50, 87
Algeria
  Algerian War, 51
  withdrawal from EC, 51, 89, 161
Allied Maritime Transport Council, 54
Asia, 8–9, 11, 109–110
association with the EC/EU
  Algeria, 51, 89, 161
  former colonies, 35, 50, 86, 89
  Greenland, 89, 161
  overseas territories, 2
  Turkey, 137, 167
  Ukraine, 169
asylum policy, 138, 140–141, 154–160
  Dublin Regulations, 106
  and Schengen Agreement, 105–106, 157
austerity, 145, 148, 151–153, 178
Austria, 48, 114–115, 123, 157

Balcerowicz, Leszek, 121
Balcerowicz Plan, 121
Belgium, 17, 46, 108, 132

colonialism, 34, 83
  economic performance, 39, 101
Benelux states, 14, 24–25, 31
Beyen, Johan Willem, 28, 34
Blair, Tony, 124, 173
Bolkestein, Frits, 132
Bolkestein Directive, 132–133
Brandt, Willy, 57, 60
Bretton Woods institutions, 55, 61, 67
Briand, Aristide, 12, 15
Brussels effect, 111, 177
Bush, George, 90

Cameron, David, 161
Camps, Miriam, 7
Canada, 175
capitalism, 192
Cassis de Dijon ruling, 79
China, 111–112, 168, 170, 172, 175, 184
Chirac, Jacques, 99, 109, 173
Churchill, Winston, 188
Cissé, Madjiguène, 106
Cold War, 14, 19, 30, 85, 89, 98, 191
  as a factor, 15, 19, 23, 26, 29, 37, 63, 71, 115
  and neutrality, 19, 114–115
  as a period, 16, 36, 62
  colonies, 11, 16, 35, 50, 83, 86, 89
  colonial wars, 36, 51
  decolonisation, 37, 50–51

243

Index

Common Agricultural Policy (CAP), 43–45, 58–59, 67, 90
   creation, 34–35, 42–43
   and disintegration in the EC, 43, 60, 112–113
   as a social policy, 42, 44–45
Common Foreign and Security Policy (CFSP), 89, 91, 107–108
Common Market, 35, 58, 69, 71. *See also* European Economic Community (EEC)
   creation and development, 7, 31, 34, 40, 78
   economic impact, 41–42, 67, 69
   public opinion, 38
common transport policy, 34
Conference on Security and Cooperation in Europe (CSCE), 62, 64, 70, 117
Copenhagen criteria, 118
Costa v. ENEL ruling, 48
Coudenhove-Kalergi, Count Richard, 11, 15
Council of Europe, 18, 29, 36, 63, 69, 71, 83, 187
   human rights, 17, 55, 87
   organisational set-up, 20, 33, 117
   relationship to EC, 54, 66, 69–70, 73, 78, 83
   Western cooperation, 20–21
Council of Ministers
   decision-making mechanisms, 51–52, 80
   early history, 32, 51–52
   and other EC institutions, 63, 82, 108
Couve de Murville, Maurice, 52
Covid-19 pandemic, 140, 149, 174, 178, 180, 190, 192

De Gasperi, Alcide, 27–28, 30
de Gaulle, Charles, 49, 52–53, 57, 74
decolonisation, 50–51
Delors, Jacques, 77, 90, 128, 131
Denmark, 48, 88, 124
   accession to EC, 48, 58, 82
   economic performance, 76
   Greenland, 88–89
détente, 62
development policy, 50, 86–87, 109–110, 138
Draghi, Mario, 149, 153
Dulles, John Foster, 37

Economic and Monetary Union (EMU), 58, 90, 97–98, 104, 149, 178
Egypt, 36
empty chair crisis, 52–53, 140
enlargement of the EC/EU, 48, 51, 59, 88, 92–93, 95, 112, 114–116, 118, 120, 137, 168
   1973 enlargement – Denmark, Ireland, UK (and Norway), 48–49, 58, 60, 65, 69, 76–77, 82, 84
   1981 enlargement – Greece, 84
   1986 enlargement – Spain, Portugal, 84–85
   1990 enlargement – former GDR, 85, 115
   1995 enlargement – Austria, Finland, Sweden, 114–115
   2004 enlargement, 60, 117, 118–120, 122
   2007 enlargement – Bulgaria and Romania, 97, 119, 122
   2013 enlargement – Croatia, 167
Eurafrica, 50
Euratom, 32–34, 37–38, 53, 68, 90

Index

euro, 90, 97–98, 100–106, 134, 138
euro crisis, 140, 145–150, 152–156, 162, 177–178, 185, 193
European Central Bank (ECB), 97–98, 101–102, 149, 153
European Coal and Steel Community (ECSC)
  contribution to peace, 21–22, 26
  creation, 24–25, 28
  economic role, 25, 34
  relationship to other international organisations, 24, 32–34, 37
European Commission, 86, 127, 148, 151, 165, 167
  human rights, 86, 109
  and other EC institutions, 52–54, 108, 130–131
  and support for European integration, 40, 78, 84, 118, 128, 164, 189
European Council, 63–64, 108, 125, 130
European Court of Justice (ECJ), 48, 71, 73, 79, 189
European Currency Unit (ECU), 97
European Defence Community (EDC), 25, 27, 30, 37
European Economic Community (EEC), 38–45, 48–51, 53. *See also* Common Market; treaties, EEC treaty
  creation and development, 32–33
European flag, 83, 141, 152
European Free Trade Association (EFTA), 48–49, 115
European Green Deal, 189

European law, 48, 79
European Monetary System (EMS), 97, 99
European Neighbourhood Policy, 109, 168–169
European Parliament, 119, 127–128, 130–131, 148–149, 164, 179, 189
  comparison to other parliamentary assemblies, 33, 66
  first direct elections, 64, 66
  and human rights, 66
  and other EC institutions, 33, 66, 80, 130–131
European Political Cooperation (EPC), 62–64, 80, 107
European security and defence policy, 108–109
European Stability Mechanism (ESM), 147–149, 153
Eurozone, 97, 100, 102, 145–147, 149

Finland, 114, 146
Fouchet Plans, 53
France, 16–17, 34–38, 52–53, 70, 74, 123, 173–174. *See also* Couve de Murville, Maurice; de Gaulle, Charles; empty chair crisis; Fouchet Plans; Giscard d'Estaing, Valéry; Monnet, Jean; Schuman, Robert
  colonialism, 34, 36, 51
  Constitutional Treaty, 125–126, 134
  economic performance, 42, 102, 132, 147, 154
  Franco-German reconciliation, 12, 21, 27, 29, 35, 53, 99

245

Index

France (cont.)
 support for European integration, 24, 35, 39, 124, 135
 transatlantic relations, 25, 37, 53, 109
 Frontex, 105, 159

General Agreement on Tariffs and Trade (GATT), 49, 73, 76, 110, 112, 174
 Kennedy Round, 50
 Uruguay Round, 110
Germany, 16, 35, 38, 70, 85, 89–90, 108, 116, 123, 152, 157, 160. *See also* Adenauer, Konrad; Brandt, Willy; European Central Bank (ECB); Kohl, Helmut; Merkel, Angela
 colonialism, 16
 division and reunification, 15–16, 19, 85, 89–90, 98–99, 115, 123
 economic performance, 22, 24, 35, 101–102, 132, 154
 Franco-German reconciliation, 12, 21, 27, 29, 35, 53, 99
 German question, 16
 rearmament, 22, 25–27, 29
 security, 16, 25, 29–30, 116
 support for European integration, 24, 35–36, 38–39, 135
 Western cooperation, 70, 152
Giscard d'Estaing, Valéry, 67, 125
globalisation, 18, 62, 76, 79, 96, 105, 115, 134, 138, 163, 175, 184
Greece, 88, 95, 146, 151
 accession to EC, 84
 debt crisis, 140, 147–148, 150–152
 economic performance, 76, 101–102, 120, 145, 147, 154
Greenland, 88–89
Group of Six (G6), 70

Hague summit, 57–59
Hallstein, Walter, 40, 46, 52
Havel, Václav, 116
Helsinki Process, 62–63
Hitler, Adolf, 13
Hoffman, Paul G., 7. *See also* Marshall Plan
human rights, 66, 84, 86, 107, 109, 118
Hungary, 85, 117–118, 156, 160, 164

intergovernmentalism, 20, 52–53, 63–64, 91, 93, 107–108, 125, 149, 185
Ireland, 48, 58, 82, 88, 114, 124, 132, 146
 Brexit, 161–162
 economic performance, 76, 102, 145, 147
Israel, 36, 62
Italy, 70, 88, 108, 146
 colonialism, 35
 economic performance, 42, 99–102, 145, 147, 154
 support for European integration, 24, 27, 38, 135

Japan, 68, 70
 relations with EU, 111, 175
Juncker, Jean-Claude, 148, 164

Kalniete, Sandra, 119
Karamanlis, Konstantinos, 84
Keynesianism, 76

Index

Klaus, Václav, 121, 135
Kohl, Helmut, 90–91, 99, 104, 116
Korean War, 22, 25
Kurdi family. *See also* migration
Kurdi, Alan, 155–156

Latin America, 110
Le Pen, Marine, 162
Leyen, Ursula von der, 66, 167, 189
Libya, 169
Lomé Convention, 86
Luxembourg, 17, 106, 132, 149
Luxembourg compromise, 52, 80

Macken, Fidelma, 66
Macron, Emmanuel, 142
MacSharry Reform, 112
Mansholt, Sicco, 42
Marshall Plan, 7, 17
Merkel, Angela, 146, 150, 152, 172, 178
Middle East, 36, 61–62, 64, 168, 172
migration, 106, 138, 140, 154–160
Mitterrand, François, 76, 90, 99, 116
monetary policy, 61, 67, 80, 88, 101, 104, 153, 178–179
Monnet, Jean, 22, 25, 28, 30, 34, 53–54, 182
and Schuman plan, 22

Nasser, Gamal Abdel, 36
National Socialism, 12–14, 16
neoliberalism, 79, 96, 122, 133–134, 154, 175
Netherlands, 17, 24, 35
colonialism, 35, 86
Constitutional Treaty, 126–127, 134
economic performance, 24–25, 34, 133, 152, 178
support for European integration, 35, 42, 84, 91

transatlantic relations, 108
neutrality, 19, 114–115
Nixon, Richard, 62
North Atlantic Treaty Organization (NATO), 29, 33, 55, 64, 69, 84, 107, 170–171
after the Cold War, 117–118, 172
and German rearmament, 29–30
Norway, 48, 58, 105, 114, 185

Orbán, Viktor, 163
Organisation for Economic Co-operation and Development (OECD), 69, 84
organisational set-up, 71, 73
relationship to EC, 41, 69, 117
Organisation for European Economic Co-operation (OEEC), 17, 24, 29, 54
organisational set-up, 20
relationship to EC, 41
Western cooperation, 17, 48–49

pan-European Union, 11
Papandreou, Vasso, 66
Pleven, René, 25
Poland, 105, 117–119, 121, 135, 160, 164–165
Pompidou, Georges, 57–58, 60
Poos, Jacques, 107
populism, 140–141, 151, 158–159, 162–166, 192, 194
Portugal, 48, 95, 146
accession to EC, 84
economic performance, 76, 120, 145, 147
Prodi, Romano, 131

247

Index

protectionism, 34, 43, 78, 106, 113, 171–172, 174
Putin, Vladimir, 162, 164, 169, 180, 191

qualified majority voting, 51, 80

Russia, 11, 111, 116, 164, 166, 169–170
  economic sanctions against, 171
  invasion of Ukraine, 140, 170–171, 174, 189, 191
  security threat, 169–172, 184, 186, 191

Saint Malo Declaration, 173
  See also strategic autonomy
Santer, Jacques, 131, 138
Schengen Agreement, 88, 104–107, 126, 135, 157
Schuman, Robert, 21–24, 30
Schuman plan, 21–23
Second World War, 13–14, 16, 21
Single European Act (SEA), 78, 80–81, 87, 107, 126–127
Single Market, 78–80, 90, 100, 106, 134, 162, 177
Solana, Javier, 108
Soviet Union, 14, 16–18, 36, 85, 89, 118. *See also* Cold War
  economic performance, 112, 115
  global role, 17
  interaction with EC, 15, 30, 85
  views of EC, 18, 85, 118
Spaak, Paul-Henri, 27–28, 30
Spain, 95, 108, 146, 151
  accession to EC, 84–85
  economic performance, 76, 102, 145, 147, 149, 154

Spinelli, Altiero, 14
Spitzenkandidat process, 167
strategic autonomy, 173–174, 179
Suez crisis, 36, 191
supranationalism, 19–20, 51–52, 74, 82, 90–91, 100, 148–149, 180, 183, 185, 191
Sweden, 48, 114, 123–124, 132, 160
Switzerland, 48, 105, 114, 168, 190

terrorism, 88, 112, 139, 158
Thatcher, Margaret, 74, 90
  and German unification, 90
  Single Market, 74, 79
  stance on European Integration, 74, 90
Tito, Josip Broz, 15
trade barriers, 24, 40, 79
trade unions, 30, 93, 179
treaties
  Constitutional Treaty, 83, 125–126, 132, 138
    referendums, 125–126
  Draft Treaty Establishing the European Union, 27, 125–126
  ECSC treaty, 44
  EEC treaty, 34, 40, 44–45, 50–51
  Maastricht Treaty, 78, 89, 92, 94–95, 106–108, 126, 128, 130
    contents, 93, 98, 101, 104, 128, 144
    ratification difficulties, 91, 124, 132
  Merger Treaty, 51, 53
  Treaties of Rome, 35, 51, 53, 129, 191. *See also* Common Market; Euratom

Treaty of Amsterdam, 126, 128, 130
Treaty of Lisbon, 83, 126–127, 132, 146, 168
   Article 7, 164
   Spitzenkandidat process, 167
Treaty of Nice, 125–126
trial and error, 14–22, 29
Trump, Donald J., 162, 171–176, 180
Tunisia, 168
Turkey, 66, 137, 159–160, 166, 168
Tusk, Donald, 105, 165

Ukraine, 140, 169–171, 186, 192
   association with the EU, 169, 171
   Russian aggression against, 170–171, 174, 180, 189, 191
   solidarity, 170
United Kingdom, 16–17, 31, 36, 48, 58, 70, 74, 77, 79, 86, 88, 90, 95, 108, 116, 124, 128, 133, 135, 190
   accession to EC, 48–49, 57–58, 84
   Brexit, 124, 140, 161–163, 171–172, 185, 188–189, 192–194
   colonialism, 36
   economic performance, 76, 99
   European Monetary System (EMS), 68, 88, 90–91, 99
United Nations, 180
   role in global cooperation, 187
United Nations Economic Commission for Europe (UNECE), 16–18, 20, 24, 41, 54
   organisational set-up, 16–17
   relationship to EC, 18, 41, 54
   role in global cooperation, 18
United States of America, 19, 22, 25, 36–37, 62, 70, 84, 111–112, 170, 172, 176. *See also* Cold War
   economic performance, 61, 144, 180
   and European integration, 7, 37, 90
   role in Western cooperation, 17, 19, 30, 70, 107–109
   and Schuman plan, 22
   trade, 112–113, 175
   Trump presidency, 162, 172–176, 180
United States of Europe, 30

van Gend & Loos ruling, 48, 71
Van Hoof, Renée, 46
Varoufakis, Yanis, 151
Veil, Simone, 64–66

Waigel, Theo, 99
Warsaw Pact, 115
Western European Union (WEU), 17, 24, 33, 54, 66
   organisational set-up, 17
   relationship to the EC/EU, 54, 66
   security policy, 29
Wilders, Geert, 162
World Bank, 55, 121
World Trade Organization (WTO), 110, 174, 175

Yanukovych, Viktor, 169
Yaoundé Convention, 50, 86
Yom Kippur War, 62, 64
Yugoslavia, 15, 107, 139–140, 173–174

For EU product safety concerns, contact us at Calle de José Abascal, 56–1°,
28003 Madrid, Spain or eugpsr@cambridge.org.

www.ingramcontent.com/pod-product-compliance
Lightning Source LLC
LaVergne TN
LVHW011811060526
838200LV00053B/3736